Learning to Run

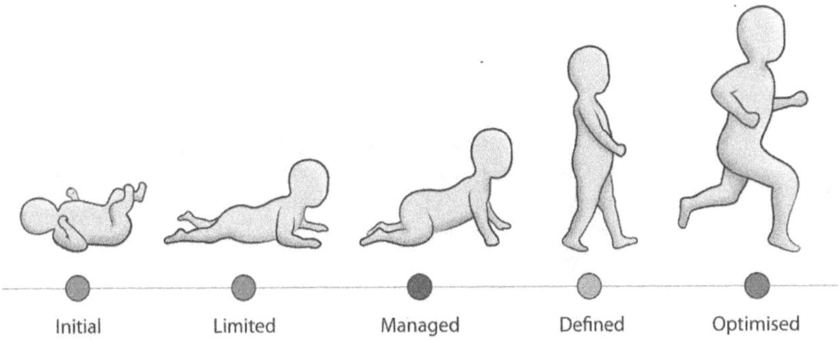

A guide to Business Process Re-engineering.
A capability maturity model to help understand
the cultural impact of change. What's going
to happen, why, and what to do about it.

By David Broadbent

Grosvenor House
Publishing Limited

This book is published by
Grosvenor House Publishing Ltd
28-30 High Street, Guildford, Surrey, GU1 3EL.
www.grosvenorhousepublishing.co.uk

A CIP record for this book
is available from the British Library

ISBN 978-1-908596-90-1

To my wife Sally, and my children Sarah, Matthew, Kirstie and Rebecca for their unfaltering love and support, without which this book would never have been finished.

Table of Contents

Images and Tables of Figures

1 Foreword

David Broadbent presented a case study at the European conference for Business Process Management 'The BPM Think Tank', hosted by the Object Management Group in November 2008 in Putten, The Netherlands.

After the presentation a number of those present suggested that David put his theories into a book. These theories explain how 'Culture' is often seen as an afterthought or the 'forgotten variable' in change programmes, and how organisations often get too ambitious to begin with and don't fully appreciate the level of maturity of their organisation to carry out change.

The impact of culture is huge and change programmes will not have the same success without changes to culture. Just introducing a new piece of software and expecting the organisation to miraculously change 'by itself' is seriously flawed

Lots of organisations suffer from some or all of the following issues:

- No cross-functional communication or co-operation
- No understanding of the end-to-end process
- No ownership of the end-to-end process by senior management
- No understanding of the business process capability maturity model, or where they are on that model
- Blame culture
- Silo mentality
- Resistance to change

This book split into two halves:

Part one will take a reader who is attempting business process re-engineering for the first time through the history, mechanics and standards used to map and analyse processes. It takes the reader through the Samakira capability maturity model for business process re-engineering and has exercises to establish where your organisation currently sits on that learning curve. Lastly, it introduces the reader to the Samakira Change Cycle, which is a simple approach to complex change programmes.

Part two is a narrative based on the presentation David delivered initially at the OMG (Object Management Group) 'BPM Think Tank Conference' in Putten in the Netherlands in 2008, then expanded on these theories at the OMG international twentieth anniversary conference in San Antonio, Texas in September 2009. This takes the reader through not only the stages of process change, but the typical cultural issues listed above and how they were overcome. So if you have a grounding in business process change, part two might be of more significance than part one, but there may well be some pieces of use as reminders.

In a nutshell, the recipe for tackling business process change is to take a dollop of determination, a main order of intelligence, a side order of common sense and a sprinkling of humour. If you do this, many things are possible.

2 Acknowledgements

I would like to thank Miss Kirstie Broadbent for assisting and creating images for this book. Also I would like to thank Mr. Benjamin Buchanan for creating the cover image.

Additionally, for this book I have referred to pieces of information from many great writers and thinkers who have studied 'Change'. I would like to thank the following for their permission to reproduce copyright material:

Gartner – The 'Meeting the challenge: the 2009 CIO agenda' paper, published January 2009 and the latest CIO Agenda survey published January 21st 2011

Professor Michael Hammer and Dr John Champy – 1993 Re-Engineering the Corporation.

2008 Logica and the Economist Intelligence Unit report on business process re-engineering, Professor W.H. Keesomlaan of Logica Management Consulting, entitled 'Securing the value of business process change'.

'Business Process Re-Engineering a Consolidated Methodology' published in 1999 by Subramanian Muthu, Larry Whitman and S. Hossein Cheraghi of the Department of Industrial and Manufacturing Engineering – Wichita State University – Wichita United States of America.

Object Management Group (OMG) – Business Process Modelling Notation (BPMN) – www.omg.org

Bruce W. Tuckman – Groups Development – Forming, Storming, Norming, Performing.

Donald H Rumsfeld – USA Secretary for Defence – 'Unknown unknowns' Feb 12, 2002, Department of Defence news briefing.

Albert Einstein – 'Level of thinking' quote.

Charles Darwin – 'Survival' quote.

BPMN – Modelling and Reference Guide – Stephen A White PhD & Derek Miers.

Anne Salerno & Lillie Brock – The interchange cycle. Reprinted with permission of the publisher from The Change Handbook copyright© by Salerno and Brock, Berrett-Koehler Publishers, Inc. San Fancisco, CA

Suzanne Robertson – Extracts from 'An early start to testing: How to test requirements'.

The Definitive Book of Body Language – Allan & Barbara Pease.

3 Glossary

The following table is a glossary of terms used in this book.

Term	Definition
Application	Software used to run the processes
BA	Business Analyst
BPCMM	Business Process Capability Maturity Model
BPEL	Business Process Executable Language
BPM	Business Process Management
BPMN	Business Process Modelling Notation
BPR	Business Process Re-Engineering
CMDB	Configuration Management Database
CMS	Configuration Management System
Data	Data architecture describes the data structures used by a business and/or its applications
DRIP	Data Rich Information Poor
ERP	Enterprise Resource Planning
ITIL	Information Technology Infrastructure Library
LAN	Local Area Network
OMG	Object Management Group
PAT	Portable Application Testing
PCA10	Percentage of Calls Answered in 10 seconds
PID	Project Initiation Document
PRINCE	Projects in a controlled environments
Process drawing	A process drawing is the capturing of an ordered sequence of business activities and supporting information that describe how a business pursues its objectives
RACI	Responsible, Accountable, Consulted, Informed – role descriptions
SME	Subject Matter Experts
System	Hardware – Laptops, Desktops, Servers, Networks, Printers
UAT	User Acceptance Testing
WAN	Wide Area Network
WfMC	Workflow Management Coalition

4 Introduction

4.1 Introducing 'Cultural Change' by David Broadbent

Change has always been a requirement in business, but it seems to be a necessity for all organisations at the moment. The worst economic performance of companies across many sectors has many analysts describing the global economy on the verge of somewhere between 'Recession' and 'Depression' depending on the business sector.

Organisations used to consider that 'Organisational Change' was something that they may have wanted to do. Now organisations ***have*** to change. They have had to reduce their costs, which sometimes means that they have to reduce the number of staff they have, yet within this environment they still have to deliver the services that they are contracted to deliver to their customers. So when people leave, they are not being replaced. This puts additional work and stress on those that are left. The need for efficiencies becomes paramount. Unemployment rises, so those that have jobs want to keep them, and fear of losing your job adds yet more stress to the workplace. So a stressed workforce, having to do more work with less people, is not a good recipe for a productive organisation.

In the public sector the global recession has left many countries with deficits running into the hundreds of millions. This state of affairs will result in hundreds of thousands of public sector roles being either cut completely or the number of people doing the role will need to be reduced. This has already began to happen in the United Kingdom with redundancies in the armed forces and for the first time redundancies in Police forces.

I write this not as some form of scaremongering, but to help set the scene, because at the heart of every organisation is its people. When organisations go through 'change' many factors are taken into consideration, but more often than not, its people are not, or not sufficiently.

This book will look at not only the mechanics of change but also the impacts on the culture of an organisation as it goes through change. These observations are based on the various organisations that I have worked with, worked in and studied over 30 years in a variety of business sectors both public and private, and the last 14 years in the field of business process re-engineering and change management.

I will use a number of analogies to explain my theories, as this has been the most successful vehicle to explain some of the potentially complex issues in a Business Process Management Masterclass I created and run for clients.

People often fear change because of fear of the unknown, and lots of organisations are poor at communicating to their people when they are changing, what these changes will include and how it will affect them. Additionally people do not view potential changes from a corporate perspective. When the rumour mill starts churning out news that things are about to change, the first thought that will pop into a person's head is, 'how will this affect **Me**? My career, my lifestyle, my life?' And until these fears are allayed, there is the perfect environment for resistance to change to begin. Even before people know what the changes are, they are resistant to them.

In this book we will look at the following areas:

- Why businesses change. And why they sometimes change badly.
- The impacts of change on an organisation's culture.

- A capability maturity model for business process re-engineering.
- The phases of successful change.
- Common types of 'Resistance to change' and how to deal with it.

It will look at the above aspects primarily from a practical and cultural perspective.

On occasions I will refer to a Business Process Management Masterclass that I created to assist clients who were usually at the beginning of the journey in organisational change. It is a one or two day workshop that takes the attendees through how to map processes, some of the methodologies used in change management and some of the cultural issues that may face. At the time of writing over 850 people from both public and private sector companies have attended these classes and they have been a great source of information about how change has been implemented in their organisations.

At the heart of successful change is 'Common Sense'. Sometimes seen as an oxymoron due to its apparent lack of commonality, however, it is my view that a flexible common sense approach yields more results than rigid methodologies. Most of the widely used methodologies come from specific business sectors, mainly manufacturing, and are very efficient at delivering beneficial results in those sectors, but I don't believe there is a 'One Size Fits All' in terms of process management.

I believe this is the case because very few organisations are the result of a single vision of a single person carried out across an organisation from end to end. Most organisations are the result of countless decisions made by countless managers over a number of years across many departments, hopefully all for what seemed to be good business reasons at the time, but collectively don't add together because they were usually made in isolation or within the scope of only focusing on a single area of an organisation and not an end-to-end process.

The proof of this is that many times I have asked groups of senior managers, 'If I gave you a blank piece of paper and asked you to design this organisation how it should really look, would it look like it is today?' The majority of answers are a resounding 'No'.

Yet when I ask senior management, 'What metric are you trying to improve with your change programme?' many find this very difficult to articulate. Is it any wonder their staff find it difficult to understand why the changes are taking place? Is it any wonder that it is often difficult to quantify whether the exercise was value for money if you can't define the metric you're trying to improve and what improvement would be considered a success?

From a cultural perspective, Business Process Management is probably best described as 'state of mind'. Successful continuous improvement of what an organisation does comes from an attitude that doesn't see business process re-engineering as a 'one-off' exercise or project. Instead it should be a view that everyone within an organisation is always looking at what they do with the thought of 'how can we do this better' lurking at the back of their minds, and having an approach to introduce change smoothly so that the organisation is always dynamic in nature and doesn't remain static.

Part One Introduction

This book has been split into two parts. Part one will cover the history and mechanics of business process management. It will cover the needs for a standard approach and what standards should be employed. It will look at terminology and aspects of some methodologies commonly used today. It will take the reader through a business process capability maturity model that will show them where they are on the learning curve of being able to implement changes to their processes, and it will take the reader through a standard approach that will cover the major stages of the introduction and maintenance of a change programme.

Part two will demonstrate these theories being put into practice and the cultural obstacles that will have to be overcome.

5 Changing a Business

5.1 Why do businesses change?

So what is change? The Compact Oxford English Dictionary defines the verb of change as:

Change

• **verb 1** make or become different. **2** exchange for another. **3** move from one to (another). **4** (**change over**) move from one system or situation to another. **5** exchange (a sum of money) for the same sum in a different currency or denomination.

The first definition is the one we will look at in detail as that encapsulates business process re-engineering. To make or become different means that something has changed.

During the course of this book there are a number of definitions I'll give for the purposes of explanation of my theories. These are my definitions and may not necessarily be agreed with by some others, however it will put the versions of change I talk about in this book into a form of context that should be easily understood.

Definition 1 – Organisational Change (New Change) V Organisational Improvement (Ongoing Change)

Organisations change continually and one can make the assumption that if a change does not improve the organisation, why do it in the first place? But there is more than one type of 'change' and often the way these two different types of changes are tackled are also different. There is the 'New Change' which can be described as the introduction of something that never existed before within an organisation and therefore new processes have to be designed. These might need underpinning by new applications, new systems, additional or different data, new roles may need to be created and so on. This change can be seen as a 'one-off' to create something from essentially nothing.

Once something has been created it can always be improved and this is the second form of change. 'Improvement' or 'Ongoing Change' starts from the basis that processes and the things that underpin them already exist. There may be many reasons for wanting to improve a process and drivers for this type of change will be looked at in detail later. However this definition serves to highlight one of the problems in delivering any form of transformation within an organisation and that is around how it is communicated to those it will affect.

To ensure staff buy into change of either type, a great deal of communication needs to take place before, during and after the changes are implemented. The more that staff are communicated with, the less assumptions will be made. This will be discussed in detail later.

I draw your attention to this definition because the majority of this book is focused on the 'ongoing change' and is described just as 'change' rather than 'Organisational improvement'. That's not to say that the principles, tools and techniques discussed could not be used in either situation, because they can. However, I will state that in the world of 'continual improvement' change never ends and one of the problems with communicating the principle of continual improvement is that change programmes should not be seen as 'one-offs'.

Therefore, the exception to this rule would be where an organisation is introducing a 'New Process' which means the organisation has to change, but once this project is completed and the processes go live, they become existing processes and then all the principles of 'continual improvement' will apply.

Definition 2 – Business Process Re-Engineering V Business Process Management

As far back as the 1970s organisations such as Baan were investing in the creation of what was called Enterprise Resource Planning (ERP). Over the following 30 years organisations have realised that at the core of what an organisation 'does' is not necessarily its hardware or software, but its processes. This gave birth to Business Process Re-Engineering in the 1990s and early 2000s. But now organisations are beginning to realise that whereas the initial view was that these exercises were seen as 'one-off projects', business processes need to be continually monitored and updated to keep pace with the market in which the organisation operates. Consequently the term Business Process Management (BPM) will be used in this book, as you will see it is not a one-off exercise but a change in operational culture to enable 'Continual Improvement' of an organisation.

Therefore this will be referred to as happening within a 'Change Programme' rather than a project. This is because a project has a start, middle and end, but this should not end so the distinction needs to be made.

Gartner's 'Meeting the challenge 2009 CIO Agenda' report, published in January 2009, interviewed 1,526 CIOs who represent more than $138 billion in corporate and public sector IT spending. According to Gartner, two fundamental questions faced executives in 2009:

- In an uncertain economy, where should the enterprise focus its attention and resources?
- Beyond cost cutting, what are the enterprise goals in a volatile market?

See table below.

Each CIO was asked to list their top five priorities with regard to 'Business expectations for IT focus on improving current operations and performance'.

As you see from the table below, 'Improving business processes' had been top of the pile for the previous four years.

Business expectations for IT focus on improving current operations and performance

Business expectations	Ranking of business priorities CIOs selected as one of their top 5 priorities					
Ranking	2009		2008	2007	2006	2012
Improving business processes	1	↔	1	1	1	2
Reducing enterprise costs	2	↑	5	2	2	7
Improving enterprise workforce effectiveness	3	↑	6	4	*	6
Attracting and retaining new customers	4	⇩	2	3	3	3
Increasing the use of information/analytics	5	↑	8	7	6	8
Creating new products or services (innovation)	6	⇩	3	10	9	1
Targeting customers and markets more effectively	7	↑	9	*	*	9
Managing change initiatives	8	↑	12	*	*	12
Expanding current customer relationships	9	⇩	7	*	*	11
Expanding into new markets or geographies	10	⇩	4	9	*	4
Consolidating business operations	11	↑	13	14	*	15
Supporting regulation, reporting and compliance	12	↑	14	13	*	16
Creating new sources of competitive advantage	13	⇩	11	8	*	5

Top 10 Business Priorities	
Top 10 Technology Priorities	**Ranking**
Increasing enterprise growth	1
Attracting and retaining new customers	2
Reducing enterprise costs	3
Creating new products and services (innovation)	4
Improving business processes	5
Implementing and updating business applications	6
Improving technical infrastructure	7
Improving enterprise efficiency	8
Improve operations	9
Improving business continuity, risk and security	10

Figure 1 - Gartner 'meeting the challenge 2009' and CIO Agenda 2011 report

Not surprisingly the focus has moved to fiscal areas of the business. In these difficult financial times increasing growth must be a priority, as is attracting and retaining customers. But these and numbers three and four are only achievable with process.

An organisation needs to review its operational processes in the same way it views its applications and systems in terms of whether they are 'fit for purpose' and where they fit into the strategies of an organisation.

This continual improvement is driven from a number of sources. The acronym PESTLE covers many of the drivers for change:

- P – Political
- E – Economic
- S – Social
- T – Technological
- L – Legal
- E – Environmental

Some people within some public sector organisations believe that they are immune to change and evidence may show that change in the public sector can happen a lot slower than in the private sector. But they are not immune and, in the same way that private sector organisations go through 'take-overs' or 'mergers', departments in the public sector are also merged. Different political parties will come into power and want to make changes.

In times such as those we face in the early years of the second decade of the 21st century, changes for 'Economic' reasons may well be the largest driver for change. With billions wiped off the value of companies across the globe, household names like Lehman Brothers bank in the US and Woolworths in the UK were among organisations that had survived previous economic downturns and even wars, but went out of business. The foundations of capitalism have been shaken almost to the point of collapse.

In times of a global 'downturn' or even a 'recession' changes made for 'Political' reasons will have a profound effect on both public and private sector organisations. At the start of 2009

Gordon Brown, the British Prime Minister, made a number of unprecedented changes both within government and in tandem with the Bank of England. Bank base rates have not been as low since records began and the government now holds a major stake in a number of high street banks.

The Euro zone and world markets are in the grip of uncertainty as they wait to see which countries will default on their Euro-zone payments. One thing is beyond doubt; government owned organisations will have to adopt private sector levels of operational efficiencies. People who traditionally saw their jobs as 'safe' will no longer have that luxury. At recent party conferences all parties talked of tightening belts and cuts.

Advances in technology have often been at the forefront of change as applications providers and system providers continually try and increase their market share by making their products do 'more', and do it 'faster'. IBM, Oracle and Fujitsu, to name but three, are investing large sums of money in the research and development of getting seamlessly from process maps drawn in BPMN (Business Process Modelling Notation) to BPEL (Business Process Executable Language) and back, and across multiple platforms without losing attachments and other business rules within the process maps. And although there are a number of issues that need to be overcome, I forecast the creation of an industry standard to enable this to happen will be within reach within the next three to five years.

Social and environmental drivers might not get the same level of focus as some of the others, but will still have an impact in the coming years.

5.2 Why do businesses change badly?

The Panic Environment

The main reason organisations do 'change' badly is that it is done in a totally reactive manner. This is linked to the various drivers described above but the outcome is that change is delivered in what I describe as the 'Panic Environment'. Change that is carried out in an environment of panic is rarely going to be well planned or well implemented.

In a 2008 report published by Prof W.H. Keesomlaan of Logica Management Consulting and the Economist Intelligence Unit, entitled 'Securing the value of business process change', Logica surveyed 380 Western European CEOs about change projects, the problems encountered and the reasons that business process re-engineering projects are either late, over budget, fail totally, or do not deliver what was initially expected of them. The two chief reasons were: a) senior management buy-in all the way through the programme to stop day-to-day activity overtaking the programme, and b) getting staff out of their day-to-day jobs to actually work on the change programme.

It is my view that when organisations are in the 'Panic Environment', staff are often expected to introduce changes on top of doing their day jobs. This is always a recipe for disaster. Change projects, like all other projects, need to have dedicated staff and people cannot be in two places at once. The most common result of asking people to do two jobs at once is that they do neither well as they are under so much pressure to deliver, they work too many hours and inevitably the quality of what they produce suffers.

Another element of the 'Panic Environment' is the need to see instant results. This often presents itself by insufficient planning taking place. Many studies have found that one of the common reasons projects fail to deliver to time and budget is because all the factors that ultimately needed to be taken into consideration were not done so at the project's inception. Insufficient planning leads to an insufficient scope being defined and therefore the scope gets changed as the project progresses. 'Scope creep' is allowed to happen. 'Scope creep' happens when an assumption is made in the minds of either those putting the project together, or those signing off the funds to enable the project to happen. This can include the lack of a definition of terms.

Language is often used in different ways and if terms are not defined, assumptions will be made. For example, a common misconception is the term 'System'. To an IT person a 'system' is a piece of hardware, a PC, a laptop, a server, a printer, part of the network and so on. To a non-IT person a 'system' is often misconstrued as what appears on their PC. What appears on a PC are applications. On many occasions management will say, 'We're getting a new system that will do...' and they go on to describe what their new application will do.

To an IT person an 'application' is the software that runs on the systems and the two are completely different. Therefore it is vital that in the scope section of a change project initiation document is a definition of what is 'out of scope' in as much detail as what is 'in scope'. This will be looked at in more detail later.

No end-to-end owners

Another major impact of the Panic Environment is that all parts of the organisation are told to 'become more efficient' without a concerted cross-functional consensus of ***what*** should be tackled and ***how***. This either leads to a silo mentality, or increases it if it already existed in the first place. The biggest problem with each area of an organisation introducing changes simultaneously without any co-ordination between them, is that one area may make changes that seem to make good business sense to that area of the organisation, but consequently adversely affect another part of the organisation to the extent that it directly affects delivery. The ultimate outcome is that the total organisation becomes less efficient, which is exactly the opposite of what was trying to be achieved.

Very few organisations appoint 'owners' of cross-functional critical business processes. These are processes that run across multiple departments and are fundamental to an organisation being able to operate. It seems odd that something this business critical is not given the same level of focus as organisational hierarchy. More often than not the root of the problem lies in managers only being willing to have the responsibility and accountability for things within their direct control, and cross-functional end-to-end processes will never fall into this category.

For example, all of us started the job we are doing today on our first day. To be productive on our first day, we would require the following:

- A desk
- A telephone
- A PC or laptop
- All the relevant applications I require loaded on the PC or laptop
- We would have been added to the Active Directory of the organisation, so we can use all corporate applications
- We would have appointments already in our diaries

All this adds up to you being 'productive' from day one. When I run a business process management Masterclass, I ask attendees how many of them had all of the above on their first day. Usually I get less than ten percent raising their hands.

When an organisation moves into the 'panic environment', the negative factors that affect an organisation's culture increase. These factors include things like: blame culture, lack of cross-functional communications, political in-fighting and so on. These will be looked at in greater detail later.

There are many methodologies for the implementation of change projects that, although efficient, can too often be seen as too bureaucratic and/or time-consuming.

There is a common analogy within organisations that they cannot afford to do things 'right' because they are under time pressures, yet in reality it appears they can often afford to do things at least twice, if not more, because they didn't do them right in the first place. Change projects either fail, or are over-budget and late. This appears to happen time and time again. Managers driven by short-term targets, are too preoccupied with the 'just fix it' and 'fire fighting' mentalities that the best they will achieve is to paper over the cracks and possibly make things worse in other parts of the company because they have not fully investigated the impacts of the changes they are going to make in their department.

It is my belief that another reason organisations struggle with 'change' is they don't have a full understanding of how mature their organisation is in its ability to change what they do. This leads us to the subject of their capability to change and the business process capability maturity model.

6 Business Process Capability Maturity Model

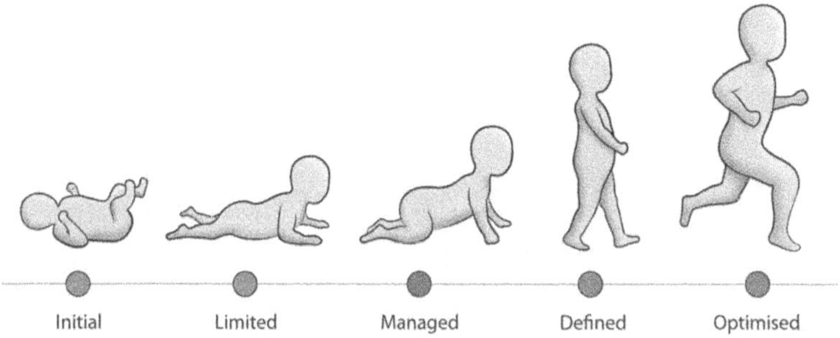

Figure 2 – Business Process Capability Maturity Model [BPCMM]

The analogy I use to explain the BPCMM is a child learning to walk and eventually run, and hence the name of the book. When a child is a baby, it cannot run, walk or even crawl. It is totally dependent on external assistance. Now, nobody would put a pair of running shoes on a baby that can't even crawl and expect it to run. Yet in organisations across the world there are people who will implement a new piece of software with little or no regard to things like: business processes, system architecture, data architecture, roles and responsibilities, or people. And just because they have implemented a new piece of software, they 'expect' the business to be magically more efficient.

One client I worked with had been to a conference and, as a result of a dazzling presentation, decided that all their organisation required was Microsoft SharePoint and then everything would be efficient. Nobody gave a thought to the huge amount of time and effort that would be required to cleanse their existing data, decide what they wanted on the SharePoint website, decide the structure of the website, decide the metadata tags for each type of document, build the website, train everyone to use it, and finally migrate the data from the existing locations into the new website. They had put the trainers on the baby and were surprised when it didn't jump up and run.

So, let's go through the various stages and how we will measure them:

6.1 Initial

The baby
The baby is lying on its back, its arms and legs flailing about. It has never walked, so realistically wouldn't have any idea how to, nor would it have the co-ordination to be able to. It is totally dependent on external assistance.

The business
The organisation that has never attempted business process engineering may not be flailing its arms and legs about, but it will not have the co-ordination across multiple functions to carry out the process without external expertise. It may be one where all 'change' is driven solely by IT. That's not to say that IT departments are not capable of change, of course they are. But although most have something to do with IT, not all processes are IT related, there are:

- Person-to-application processes
- Application-to-application processes
- Application-to-person processes
- Person-to-person processes

And in all the organisations I have come across, the majority of knowledge to run internal processes lies within people's heads, so is not stored in the IT and the person-to-person processes are usually key to the end-to-end processes.

Plenty of organisations have invested in structured approaches such as ITIL (the Information Technology Infrastructure Library). Part of ITIL is what is known in version 2 as the CMDB (Configuration Management Database), or CMS (Configuration Management System) in version 3. This is meant to hold information on what it calls 'Configuration Items' and an item can equal a piece of software, hardware, people or their locations; the purpose being that if you know what you have and where it is, then changing it should be easy. However it doesn't hold processes, so fully grasping why you do something would not be possible in ITIL, and consequently the impact of not doing something might not be known until you do it, which might be disastrous.

So in this case, external assistance would be required to:

- Help establish the goals of the change programme
- Agree the metrics to be improved
- Secure the senior management buy-in for resource and funding
- Facilitate the mapping and analyses of existing processes
- Take the client through the creation of the programme to get from the 'As Is' to the 'To Be'

6.2 Limited

The baby
This is the stage when the baby flips over from on its back to being on its front. It has to be able to do this before it can crawl, then walk, then run. The first time a baby does this, the parents don't know whether it is by accident or by a co-ordinated use

of limbs. Yet the more it does it, the better it gets at it and sooner or later it moves on to crawling.

The business
The first few time changes are introduced, there may be successes and there may be failures. The most common problem is the day-to-day business just overtakes the efforts to map, measure and re-engineer the operational processes. Work doesn't get done, or gets rushed, or the organisation gets over-ambitious and can't deliver. External assistance is still required at this stage to maintain the focus and to remind the senior management of their required commitment to the change programme without any political risks, because staff will only push their senior managers so far, because they don't want to labelled as 'disruptive'

6.3 Managed

The baby
This is the stage where the baby has started to crawl and is attempting to get to its feet. The first few times it attempts this, it can still crawl much faster than it can walk so there is the temptation, if progress is not fast enough, to drop back into crawling. External assistance is still required but it's getting less, the use of furniture or a grown-up's hand to steady them during the first steps is all it takes. So the level of independence is growing.

The business
Single departments have introduced a number of process changes and progress has been good, if not as smooth as senior management had initially hoped for. In my experience this can be due to the fact that sometimes senior management teams had not fully appreciated the impact to day-to-day operations to bring about the changes required to reach the goals set.

One problem I have come across on a number of occasions is the difficulty of actually getting people out of their day jobs long enough to re-engineer their day jobs. To set the expectation that people can carry out the work of mapping, analysing and re-engineering business processes on top of their full time day jobs, is simply not realistic. At the 2009 Gartner Business Process Management Conference, Gartner stated that the organisations that are the most proficient in delivering consistent business change are those who have been willing to invest in full time permanent change teams.

An organisation might get away with delivering the first few changes with teams doing it on top of their day jobs, by working additional hours and weekends. However, this kind of pressure cannot be maintained indefinitely and sooner or later the people working under this level of stress can burn out.

A common scenario is a department that has been good at change, for example IT, is given the responsibility to improve the efficiency of a cross-functional process like the 'New Starter' process (See fig 12)

The 'New Starter' process is a cross-functional process because it can include Operations, Finance, HR, IT, Estates, etc, to ensure that when a new starter appears on their first day, they have a desk, a PC, a telephone, all the applications they require are loaded onto the PC and dates/times for meetings are loaded into their diaries. This means that they are productive from their first day.

IT may have established a robust procedure for mapping and re-engineering processes, but the other departments either haven't got established procedures, or have not been involved in business process re-engineering before, so all the issues around silo mentality, politics, blame culture and resistance to change, etc, rear their ugly heads.

Therefore, external assistance will still be required, but it is getting less. It is more of a 'managerial' role than a 'hands-on' one. The external consultant is more engaged in tackling the cultural issues and working with senior management to remove 'blockers', that may be political or physical, rather than the actual mechanics of mapping and analysing processes.

6.4 Defined

The baby
The baby has now learned enough co-ordination and balance to walk unaided. It no longer crawls as it has realised it can reach more things standing up, and is now at a stage where it can walk just as fast as it used to crawl. It doesn't need external assistance to walk, but does need help to pick it up when it falls, which it will as it tries to move from walking to running. There will be many bruised knees and bumped heads, but perseverance will ensure that running will be achieved.

The business
The actual procedure used to re-engineer processes is fully understood in certain departments, and other departments are aware of them. A structure that holds all the critical business processes is in place to ensure that even though there are multiple projects running in parallel, no two of them are attempting to make the critical business processes do different things.

A full understanding of the end-to-end processes is now in place. Previously departments would have introduced changes that would be seen as benefits to their individual silo, but would in fact be counter-productive to a department further down the end-to-end process. This no longer happens as the end-to-end process is looked at in its entirety and is 'owned' by a senior manager.

External assistance is no longer a requirement, other than maybe to assist in the procurement of an application to hold all the process models, to review the plans to expand the scenarios in the existing models from just critical business processes to exception processes.

When Project Initiation Documents (PID) are drawn up, a section has been added where the Project Manager has to state which processes in the Business Operations Model (which holds all the processes) will be affected by their project, and how. The Business Analysts in the newly-formed permanent 'Change Team' will check the PID's to ensure that the projects are not contradicting each other in what they want the process to do.

6.5 Optimised

The baby
The baby is now matured into a child and the child has now moved from walking to running. The level of balance and co-ordination required has passed from conscious into subconscious. The child simply wants go from A to B as fast as possible and runs. If obstacles appear in its way, it will either jump over them by a short burst of increasing effort, or will run round the obstacle, which doesn't require more effort but will take longer. External assistance is no longer required, the child is independent.

The business
This is the stage where 'Change' should no longer be seen as a series of projects or a programme, rather the organisation should see itself as one where the ethic of 'Continual Improvement' drives the business. 'Change/Improvement' are seen as the norm, the way things are done in this organisation.

Goals are set in terms of the metrics the senior management want to improve. Analysis establishes the current position;

plans are drawn up to remove constraints and duplications, to bridge gaps. A structured approach that is known and fully understood right across the organisation is used to implement the plan.

If an unforeseen situation occurs due to external forces, as has happened in terms of a global recession, plans are drawn up. To overcome obstacles in the short term, additional resource may be required. Alternatively, if this is not possible, realistic expectations are set and the timescale extended.

External assistance is no longer required. The organisation is independent.

6.6 Exercise 1 – Business Process Capability Maturity Model

This exercise will help you establish where your organisation is on this Capability Maturity Model today.

Using the table in Section 12, map the end-to-end process of your organisations 'New Starter' process, from the stage where an operational department approaches Finance with a request for additional funding to pay for an extra head. I'm guessing, but I suspect HR will then be involved in sending out adverts through various media and setting up interviews. Maybe Estates will be required to sort a desk for the new starter and at some stage IT will need to be contacted to order a new PC/laptop, desk telephone, mobile telephone or Blackberry. Presumably IT will also be responsible for loading any software the new starter will require onto the systems and will need to set the new starter up on any Active Directories that are required.

As stated above, in an ideal world, when a new starter appears on their first day, they have a desk, a PC, a telephone, all the applications they require are loaded onto the PC and dates/times for meetings are loaded into their diaries, meaning that they are productive from their first day.

Once you have all of this information, you will be able to ascertain how far away in wasted staff days your organisation is currently in terms of variance from the 'ideal'.

Then ask your Finance department for an average 'cost per day/per employee' figure, which is made up of salary, pension contributions, NI, Healthcare, etc. Then multiply that figure by however many days you are away from the 'ideal' and finally multiply that figure by however many new starters your organisation had in the previous 12 months.

Example:
A company of around 400 staff has an average attrition rate of 7%, which equals 28 new starters per year, and that is a 'normal' year not a recession, which could be worse. The average salary is £30K and overhead costs are between 25%-30%, for this example we will use 30%, so the overall cost of the average member of staff is £39K.

There are 365 days per year, but in terms of 'staff days' there are only 215. This is because 104 are weekends, 11 bank holidays, 25 days' annual leave and 10 days' average sickness or training.

£39K/215 staff days = £181 cost per day.

Average time to get to a position of being 'fully productive' is 15 days.

£181 × 15 days × 28 new starters = £76,020 cost of non-conformance. Every year.

That £76K is the direct cost of doing it wrong because the end-to-end process doesn't work properly. Incidentally, when you are looking at the process 'Governance', I highly suspect you will not find a senior manager or board director who is accountable as the nominated 'Owner' of this process. That is the most common reason it goes wrong, which is odd because it is the most common process in all organisations.

This cost of non-conformance can be a powerful argument to gain buy-in of senior managers.

7 An Approach to Change

7.1 A Structured Approach

In a paper called 'Business Process Re-Engineering a Consolidated Methodology', published in 1999 by Subramanian Muthu, Larry Whitman and S. Hossein Cheraghi of the Department of Industrial and Manufacturing Engineering – Wichita State University – Wichita, United States of America, they analysed a number of methodologies that were in existence at the time and came to the conclusion that five major stages are involved within a change programme:

- Prepare for BPR
- Map and analyse As-Is processes
- Design To-Be processes
- Implement re-engineered processes
- Improve continuously

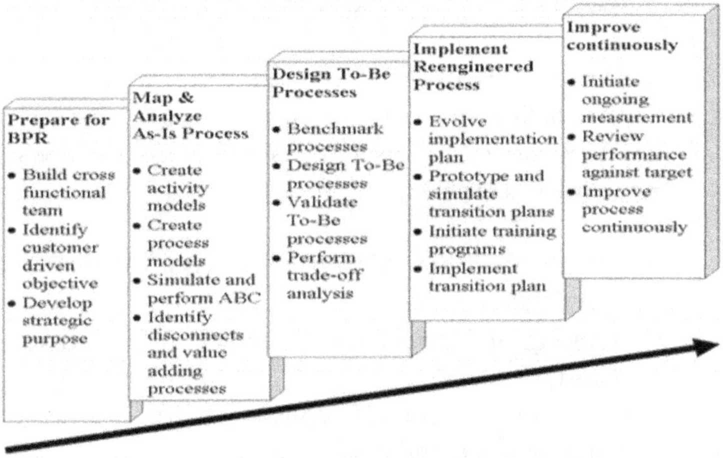
Prepare for BPR
• Build cross functional team
• Identify customer driven objective
• Develop strategic purpose
Map & Analyze As-Is Process
• Create activity models
• Create process models
• Simulate and perform ABC
• Identify disconnects and value adding processes
Design To-Be Processes
• Benchmark processes
• Design To-Be processes
• Validate To-Be processes
• Perform trade-off analysis
Implement Reengineered Process
• Evolve implementation plan
• Prototype and simulate transition plans
• Initiate training programs
• Implement transition plan
Improve continuously
• Initiate ongoing measurement
• Review performance against target
• Improve process continuously

Figure 3 – Muthu, Whitman and Cheraghi – 'Consolidated Methodology'

In 2003 Mihail Stoica, Nimit Chawat & Namchul Shin, of Pace University, New York, expanded on the work by carrying out a similar investigation and including business process re-engineering that had taken place in various institutions, both public and private sector, during the 1990s.

Their findings were that:

- 50% to 70% of re-engineering efforts fail
  - A BPR effort is considered a failure just because it doesn't provide the dramatic results it promised to deliver
- BPR is providing some vital ingredients:
  - intense customer focus
  - superior process design
  - a strong and motivated leadership
- BPR advocates strenuous hard work and instigates the people involved to not only to change what they do, but to targets altering their basic way of thinking itself
- Follow a methodology or create a new methodology
- Success of BPR may depend on the people

They therefore concluded that companies need a methodology that takes a holistic view of the organisation and that the ARMA (Agent Relationship Morphism Analysis) methodology covers all aspects of what is required.

- Agent Relationship Morphism Analysis (Valiris and Glykas 1999) combines:
- accounting BPR principles (e.g. efficiency, effectiveness and cost),
- organisational-theoretic concepts (e.g. roles and accountabilities), and
- Some powerful systematic business modelling techniques applied from IS development.

- Highlighting the importance of organisational strategy and its links to business processes throughout the redesign exercise.
- Providing a set of modelling techniques that supports the modelling of business processes.
- Taking an individualistic (employee level) and a holistic (business process level) view.
- Taking a holistic and systematic approach to BPR.

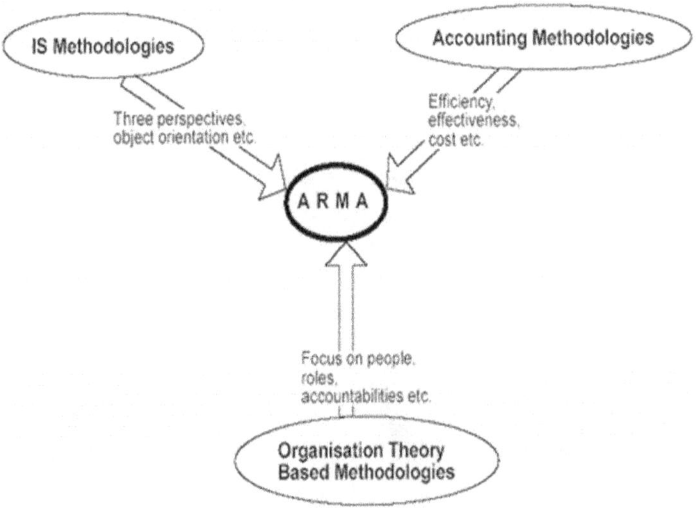

Figure 4 – Agent Relationship Morphism Analysis [ARMA]

Each of these studies was carried out prior to the global recession but, taking into account their findings and adding the almost thirty years of experience working with organisations going through change programmes, I have created the Samakira 'Change Lifecycle Model'.

Where it differs from the models above is the focus on communications. In a working environment where redundancies have been an unavoidable part of the survival of organisations, people will be working under a level of stress. This stress will be looked at more closely later in 'Resistance to change', however it is my experience that when people feel change is being imposed upon them, that is when they will resist it more. This resistance becomes more entrenched if people feel that they aren't being told what is happening and the only information coming to them is via the company rumour mill.

The most effective way to overcome this fear of change, as well as just being good practice, is to continually communicate. That is why communication is at the hub of the cycle and is linked to every stage. So then at every stage people will know what is happening.

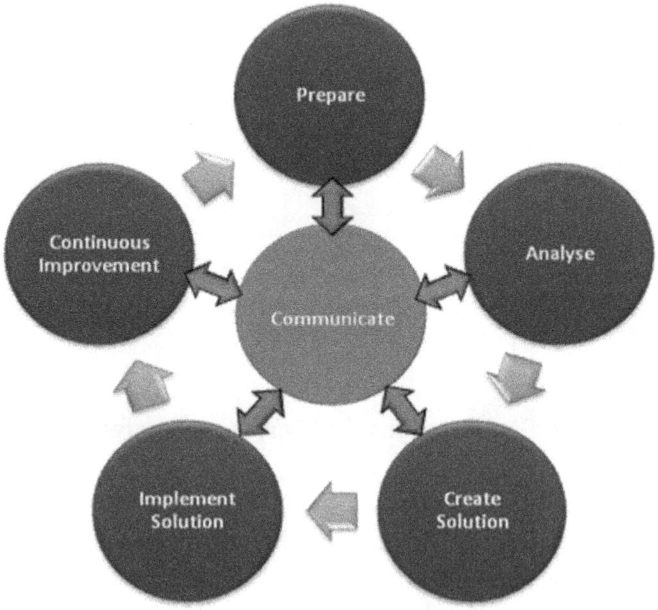

Figure 5 – Samakira Change Lifecycle Model

Each of these stages is important but preparation has to be the one that is consistently done the most poorly. This is because a lot of change introduced into organisations is reactive rather than proactive. It is implemented in a 'Panic Environment' and so insufficient time is given to preparation. However the outcome of poor preparation will invariably come back to haunt any change programme.

7.2 Preparation

7.2.1 Getting Started

The approach above sets out five clear stages. In preparation, the organisation needs to establish the goals and visions of the programme in clear quantifiable statements. This states where an organisation is trying to get to. Then process mapping and analysis will establish the current 'As Is' performance of the organisation in the same clear quantifiable metrics and statements. Only then can the organisation have a full understanding of the gap between the two and start to create the solution that will bridge that gap.

7.2.2 The Vision

A common start point is when a senior manager decides that change has to happen. Depending on where the organisation is on the capability maturity model will impact how this is approached, and there are a number of potential drivers for this, as have been described earlier. However, once the decision has been made then the start point needs to be the high level vision of where it is the organisation is aiming to get to.

There are a number of methodologies that can be used to brainstorm this goal. The important thing is that the vision can be articulated to all staff in language they understand.

Professor Michael Hammer and Dr. John Champy, in their book 'Re-Engineering the Corporation', described 'transformation' as:

> 'The fundamental rethinking and radical redesign of business processes to achieve dramatic improvements in critical contemporary measures of performance, such as cost, quality, service and speed.'

The most important part of this statement is that the goal has to be measurable. The old adage is that you can pick any two out of the following three, Cheap – Fast – Good. If you want something to be good and fast, it probably won't be cheap; if you want it to be fast and cheap, it probably won't be that good; and if you want something to be cheap and good, it probably won't be very fast. Some of the metrics naturally oppose each other; if you wanted to improve the speed of a process the cost could rise, if you wanted to decrease the cost then performance or quality may be affected.

So deciding which metric you are trying to improve will dictate the way that a process gets re-engineered. Therefore, the goal has to be defined also in terms of the metrics of where you believe you are to start with and what critical success factors would establish that the goal has been achieved.

Once this goal has been defined, then how it is communicated to the people it is going to affect is also crucial. If people are not told exactly what is going to happen during a period of change then they will make their own assumptions. Therefore, at the same time as the senior management team is creating the vision, I suggest to them that they also need to create the communications plan that will run ahead of it.

It needn't be a fully verified communications plan initially, but something that lets the staff know that change is coming and that they will be kept up-to-date as each stage is agreed. There will be reaction at each end of the scale. This may initially cause problems that will have to be overcome as there will be some for whom it will be a total shock that change is coming and there will be others who will be encouraged that outdated processes are to be reviewed and re-engineered. It may be a cliché but the way to get round this situation is to do three things: Communicate – Communicate – Communicate.

See section 7.4.6 – Communications Plan

7.2.3 Gain Buy-in

It has been shown that one of the most common problems change programmes have is having senior management buy-in for the duration of the programme. The Economist Business Unit and Logica Management Consulting published a white paper in 2008 called 'Securing the value of business process change', in which they interviewed over 380 'C' level management from private and public sectors about business change programmes.

In a section of the survey that looked at the most common reason for problems, they asked the following question:

What have been the main barriers to effective business process improvement at your company? Select up to three.

The responses in order were:

a) Pressures of day-to-day business
b) Lack of resources dedicated to the task
c) Lack of alignment between functions
d) Lack of necessary IT infrastructure/applications
e) Lack of expertise in business process design/change management
f) Lack of relevant indicators to measure/track improvements against
g) Lack of acceptance/buy-in by employees
h) Poor planning
i) Lack of support from senior management
j) Organisational change

k) Poor implementation/project management
l) Poor governance
m) Other

These findings map very neatly onto organisations at the lower end of the Business Process Capability Maturity Model (BPCMM) as the expectations they set are unrealistic. They have not taken into account the impact on day-to-day business. There is reluctance by managers to give their best staff the time away from their day jobs to work on the change programme. Commitment may be high initially but it has to be maintained, otherwise day-to-day business priorities will overtake the initial commitment. This management buy-in has to be visible and consistently communicated.

It may be an uncomfortable truth but, faced with a request to provide a resource for a change programme for a number of months that might be unavailable for their normal day job, managers have been inclined to look at who they could afford to be without for two to three months, rather than their 'Star Players'. Whether they will openly admit it or not, each manager will have their 'Star Players' and if they are asked to provide a resource for one day, then maybe the star players will be made available, but it is a huge commitment for the same people to be made available for the duration of the change programme, even though they would make the best 'Subject Matter Experts'. The people who are nominated can be one of the most visible demonstrations of senior management buy-in if their 'Star Players' are seconded into the change programme.

Therefore in the same way as any other major programme, the change programme needs to have a senior management sponsor. The change programme will need to have a programme director or manager who will be ultimately responsible for its implementation. And this individual will need to live and breathe the programme day-in and day-out until the organisation has moved up the capability maturity model. The programme may have an external business process consultant or external expertise, depending on where they are on the BPCMM. The more an organisation goes through change, the better they will get at it, the more skills transfer will take place and the less dependent on external skills an organisation will become (see Business Process Capability Maturity Model).

At their 2009 Business Process Management Conference, Gartner reported that the organisations that were the most successful at delivering consistent change were ones that had dedicated teams doing change rather than expecting people to be able to do it on top of their day jobs.

7.2.4 Scope

With the goal and the metrics defined, the next step is to define the scope. For those who have had exposure to methodologies such as PRINCE2, this would be the stage covered by the Business Case, the 'Statement of Requirements' or 'Project Mandate' documents.

When defining the scope, there should be as much attention focused on what is **out** of scope as what is **in** scope. This is often not done well and the result of this is that parties make assumptions of what should be included in the programme.

There should be no ambiguity or assumptions in the change programme. The more time and effort that is spent in this step, the greater the chance of success later. There will be less chance of 'scope creep' because one party assumed something would be included and later it therefore has to be included, but there is no additional funding or resource available.

However, it is often difficult to get all of the scope agreed and this should not hold up the programme. If only 80% of what is wanted can be defined at the inception of the programme, then that list of targets becomes the 100% of what is 'in scope'. As other requirements unfold they can be included, but under formal change control where additional resources, funding, materials and the impact on timescales can be properly defined.

The scope will also include the critical success factors and the metrics that will be used to measure the progress and completion of the initial phase of the programme. Ultimately the goal should be that at some point the programme will hand over to a newly-created change department which will own the delivery and management of change within the organisation.

7.2.5 Resources

Once the senior management sponsor/champion is on board and a programme director or owner has been appointed, the rest of the resource requirements need to be filled.

The resources required fall into three camps: Subject Matter Experts, Business Analysts and Project Support.

The first of these, the Subject Matter Experts (SME), are people who do the role today; not a manager who did the role a number of years ago. A Subject Matter Expert would be best described as someone who is working close enough to the coalface that they would be able to fully understand and communicate the potential impact of any change made to the process they use on a regular basis. Ideally a Subject Matter Expert would also be empowered by the senior management to implement the changes. If they are not given the authority to make the changes, then the management team would need to be prepared to make the time required to understand and authorise decisions as the implementation plan is developed. Another demonstration of senior management buy-in is the level of empowerment the 'Change Team' is given and that this empowerment is also communicated so the empowerment cannot be rescinded. Defining the change product categories allows the team the freedom to get on with the job of making it happen.

The second of these camps are the Business Analysts. There are pros and cons to using internal or external business analysts. Internal business analysts would usually have a good idea of the 'As is' processes, the terminology used within the business, and often they would have a good idea of the personnel they would need in a room to be able to map a process. However, there is a risk with internal business analysts that they would leap to assumptions because they were too close to a process being mapped. Just because two people work in the same department doing the same job doesn't always mean they will always do it in the same way. If only one of these people were interviewed to gain an understanding of the 'As Is', a second viewpoint may be missed. It can sometimes be difficult for internal business analysts to be impartial, after all they would usually come from one of the areas likely to be affected by the change.

External Business Analysts would have no political axes to grind. They would have no political loyalties to any area of the business, so they could be impartial. However, they would have to get up to speed on the personnel, the terminology used and the processes.

My recommendation would be that, if it is possible, a mixture of internal and external expertise is used to cover both pros and limit the cons.

The third is Project Support. This would include parts of the business such as, HR, IT, Finance, etc, and if the organisation has a formal Project Office, then this area as well. It is important to note that studies have found that organisations that approach change programmes in the same way as any other series of projects, with the same diligence and support, are those that are the most successful at implementing change. These areas of the business are already cross-functional so have a vested interest in the increases of efficiency in cross-functional end-to-end processes.

If an organisation doesn't have a programme office then it would be my recommendation to set one up and this might require external skills. It will cover definitions of change categories so the programme director knows how much empowerment and flexibility the team has. This will assure senior management the areas that require their 'rubber stamping' are done. Regular Change Advisory Board (CAB) meetings will be put into the senior management team diaries on a monthly basis and cancelled if they are not required, rather than not provisioning for the meetings then trying to find space in all the senior management diaries at a later date. This is another demonstration of management buy-in and sends an important message to staff about the commitment of the senior management team.

A communications plan will be formalised, so that following each CAB meeting a communications update will be posted using whatever media is at the organisation's disposal. Mapping applications will be looked at, space on shared drives or collaboration environments will be made available to store process maps. Locations for workshops to map processes will be made available, etc.

Level 1 drawings will be drafted so the storage architecture can start to be defined. If this can be done around a business lifecycle, so much the better (see Retail Lifecycle Model Section 9.1.1 – Fig 13).

The resources will need to work together as a team. One of the first tasks they should carry out is to give the programme an identity. This will be their identity so it should be something they can all be proud of contributing to. It will also give the management team something to communicate and it will kick off the expectation that change is coming, but it will be carried out in a structured manner so there will be fewer surprises and, therefore, less resistance to change. The team members themselves can be part of the presentations to the company stating that change is coming and taking people through the steps of the journey they are about to embark on. The team will present the Business Process Capability Maturity Model, explaining where the organisation currently is on the learning curve and the plans to get further up the curve, thereby setting realistic expectations for people about what is going to happen.

The cultural forming of the team will be looked at in greater detail later, however, pre-work carried out during the 'preparation' phase of the programme would include the identification of some cultural 'points of pain' and potential action plans to fix them. This gives the programme a level of momentum and it is widely recognised that programmes that can deliver early successes have a greater chance of overall success.

7.3 Analysis

7.3.1 Setting the level playing field

It is important that the team which will go through all the stages of change starts from the same level of understanding about how to map and analyse processes. The mechanisms used to map and analyse the organisation must be fully understood by all those it is going to affect.

To achieve this, the team will probably need some training on how to map business processes to a standard. Most organisations will have qualified Project Managers, some will have staff with ITIL qualifications, and so on. The most common problem is that organisations have insufficient skills in mapping and analysing their processes to know what it is they should be changing in the first place.

For this reason I created a Business Process Management Masterclass. Neither PRINCE2 nor ITIL cover the mapping and analysis of business processes to establish constraints, gaps and duplications within end-to-end business processes. So although these skills will be of great use when we get to the 'Implementation' stages, they are light on the process analysis work required at the start.

I recommend to clients that the Masterclass is not just for the IT department or members of staff with 'change' in their job titles, as change affects everyone and more accurate maps will be created if those being interviewed to create them can also read them. Additionally, as will be shown later, when staff are involved in the creation of a solution then there is less likely to be resistance to the implementation of that solution, because the people who created it own it. So if the staff it will affect are used to help map both the 'As Is' and the 'To Be' maps, then they will know what is happening and will be able to raise any concerns.

The Masterclass covers the background to change methodologies without dictating any particular methodology. I do not believe there is a 'one size fits all' each organisation is different and therefore the approach will need to be different. Actually I'd go as far as to say that within an organisation different projects may well require different approaches.

The Masterclass covers notation, principally BPMN (Business Process Modelling Notation), as it is an international standard for the capturing of processes and how to analyse the processes. This means that once the 'real' work begins all the parties will be able to draw maps, analyse maps and interpret any map drawn by anyone else. Other advantages of using an industry standard like BPMN is that firstly, any external expertise brought in will automatically be able to interpret what the organisation had mapped, and secondly, if at some future point the organisation decides to invest in a formal application for the mapping and management of their operational processes, maps drawn in BPMN can be imported into all the major applications.

Therefore I highly recommend that as part of project 'start up' some form of process mapping training is given to the team that will be involved in the project. This might seem an additional cost that adds little value, but in my experience the amount of time that gets lost in misinterpretation of materials outweighs this.

7.3.2 Change Champions

The group of Subject Matter Experts gathered will ultimately be the team that will carry out the mapping and analysis, and they will create the solutions to remove the constraints and duplications, and bridge the gaps. To succeed in this they must adopt a new identity, a cross-functional identity. This new identity will enable the team to move away from silo mentality and the blame culture it brings with it, to a support culture by working together. It will enable them to work together as a team as they move to a 'different level of thinking', as Einstein put it.

The term 'Change Champions' was one of the names a team I worked with decided to call themselves, to give them this different identity. What the team calls itself doesn't really matter. The important thing is that they understand they will not move forward until they have shed their silo mentality.

From a cultural aspect there is a lot of work required to get a group of Subject Matter Experts to work together as a team.

This will be investigated in more detail in the 'Journey' in part two, later in this book, however it is likely that the team will need to go through some form of the Bruce Tuckman group development stages of 'Forming', 'Storming', 'Norming' before they reach 'Performing'.

In the early stages of the programme, while the team is in the first three stages of the business process capability maturity model, they will need external experienced assistance to help them. They will be forming as a team, they will be dealing with their own resistance change and they will be dealing with changing from their role as representatives of their department or silo into the change team, to the representatives of the change team into their own department. This is a subtle change but an important one as the team creates its own identity and the barriers between the departments start to fall as the members of the group shed their 'silo identity' and take on a 'cross-functional identity'. It won't be without its challenges, as people will bring different amounts of 'baggage' with them. This is one of the reasons for having an external person, who has no political axe to grind, facilitating the group at the early stages.

They will have to overcome their own resistance to change if they want to make the change programme a success. How to tackle the various types of resistance to change will be investigated in greater detail in the second section of this book.

Exercise:
An initial exercise the group or team can do is to have an external facilitator run a session where each member of the group describes the three things that give their department the most 'pain'. I mean pain simply as the thing that is the most discussed thing that people would change if they were allowed to. I often open this session with the following statement, 'You are allowed to run your organisation for a week, you are the

boss, the CEO, the MD, whatever you like to call it, you are the top of the pile. But a week is not a long time to change anything you like, so you are only allowed three things.'

I deliberately tie them into three things, because otherwise it can quickly descend into a negative session where they just go through everything that is wrong with the organisation and people can get very depressed because everything seems to be bad and hopeless. To avoid this, in advance tell the attendees that they have the opportunity to look at creating changes either just in their department, or a cross-functional process, but only three. So they are challenged with discussing these things with the other people in the department they represent to enable them to come to the workshop armed.

Each person has about five minutes to present their 'points of pain' and, once everyone has done theirs, there will be a list on a flip chart. Then the facilitator takes the team collectively through each one and, by a show of hands, gives them a low, medium or high weighting in terms of:

- Impact/benefit
- Time to first version of product
- Cost of first version of product

Impact is in terms of how beneficial the change would be and this can be described in a number of metrics, either financially, in terms of productivity, or just that it would make people feel better. I'm aware the last one is a subjective metric and therefore hard to measure, but in the early stages it is important to get the programme some credibility and some successes. This is a major factor in dealing with resistance, so my recommendation would be to try and keep these change products as simple as possible.

Time is in terms of how long the team believes it would take, if the resources were available, to deliver the first version of the product. My recommendation would be not to be too analytical at this stage as the team is in a workshop environment. Look at time in terms of days or weeks. The facilitator will need to stress that these are not time estimates that people will be challenged on. At this stage it is just to put the list of suggestions into an order of which ones to tackle first.

Cost is in terms of resources and funding. Resource is in terms of both people and materials, whether the materials are simply some disk space to store stuff, or software, or physical items. The people aspect will be tied into the time in which it might be possible for two people to carry out a task in one week that one person might take two weeks to deliver, so there will need to be a modicum of common sense in these estimates.

Using this weighting and giving one point for low, two points for medium and three points for high in each category, it should be relatively straightforward to get your pain list into an order of priority.

Once your list is in an agreed priority order, take the top three or four 'pains' and, either collectively or breaking into breakout groups, go through in more detail what would be the final outcome, what interim versions could be delivered, and what the interim benefits would be. Once these have been presented back to the whole team, then the team can decide what it is going to tackle and how this can best be positively communicated to the organisation as a whole to create momentum at the start of the programme.

If one of the suggested change products will only affect one department, it might still be beneficial as all members of the team will have been involved so the team can be confident that the implementation of the change will not have an adverse affect on any other department, but the benefit can still be communicated. It will need to be a judgement call, but sometimes simple products within departments rather than cross-functional products might be easier to achieve, but they will have less impact. If something can be found that would be simple, but will benefit the maximum number of staff, that should be first.

7.3.3 Unknown unknowns

On the 12th of February, 2002, Donald Rumsfeld, the then USA Secretary for Defence, stated in a news briefing that:

'As we know, there are known knowns. We also know there are known unknowns. That is to say, we know there are some things we do not know. But there are also unknown unknowns, the ones we don't know we don't know.'

This was received with amusement by the press at the time. Yet it is an accurate statement in terms of business analysis. The scope of the programme will have been set out in the scoping document, and all assumptions raised will have been investigated. But there still may be things that will be uncovered that no-one had forecast. Some of these may be placed 'out of scope' and will be returned to in a later project, but if some of them unavoidably have to be dealt with then formal change control should be used; namely additional resource and funding is made available to support the expansion of scope. However, I'd recommend that this be resisted if possible otherwise you may find yourself on the slippery slope of 'scope creep' and the programme will just be tasked with more than it can realistically achieve with the available resource.

7.3.4 What to Analyse?

It is important to fully understand the composition of an organisation and its processes before it is changed. There are some schools of thought which counter that there is little point in spending the time, effort and money mapping processes you're about to change. However, I would beg to differ with this view. I would pose the question, How do you establish the requirements for getting from A to B if you cannot fully define where A is? You must have a good understanding of your start point in terms of process, applications, systems, data, roles and so on, to fully understand what has to be changed to get you to your goal.

Only after an understanding of where an organisation currently 'is' has been established, can an accurate forecast of the time, cost and resource requirements be made to implement the changes required.

Business Impact Assessments will also need to be carried out. In later chapters we will discuss the detailed components that can be affected by a change programme, and this information will help define the level of detail the impact assessments will need to go to. But at the outset it is important to establish the 'lenses' through which you will view change. A process may have different internal and external customers. For the external customers the change may be minimal but for internal customers it may be huge, so the needs of each needs to be understood.

For example, one project I was involved in was with a retail client who was migrating 3.8 million customers from five different trading applications onto one new trading application that would handle account start-up, account management, order taking, delivery of goods, return of goods, etc. From the internal customers' perspective, the changes were huge and affected the customer service teams, the supply chain teams, the web design and internet management teams. The primary objective of the project was that, from the external customers' point of view, the migration was 'seamless' and they should only notice that the website looked like it had been given a refresh, was easier to navigate around and responded faster.

So the business impact assessment had to look at change to the processes, applications, systems, data, roles, etc, through the 'lenses' of both internal and external customers because the 'impact' varied depending on the lens the business analyst was looking though.

The following diagram may help. If you are going to create a business impact assessment document that will cover process, applications, systems, data, roles and responsibilities multiplied by suppliers, customers and staff multiplied by three business units. Your document should have forty five sections

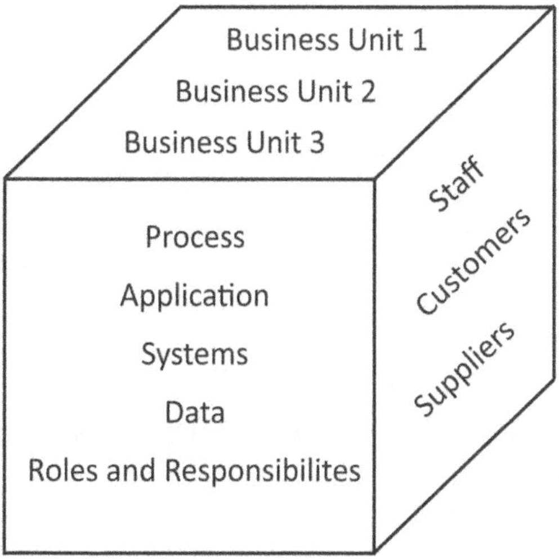

Figure 6 – Business Impact Assessment Cube

It might seem obvious common sense that if you haven't analysed the impact through all the required lenses, you will not be prepared for the issues that will arise. In my experience extra time taken planning is never wasted.

So what do you analyse? The scope will have given you an overview of the goal, the metrics and a number of high level business processes. To analyse these processes you will need to understand who does what, when, where, why and how. The John A. Zachman framework established in the 1980's as a method for establishing what was held within an 'Enterprise Architecture', is still one of the most straightforward ways of starting to understand a process. If you know who does what, when, why, where and how, then you must have a good understanding of the process and what underpins the process.

WHO: This will include the roles that carry out the process, the roles that supply information that the process requires, the role or roles that the process supplies information to, and the roles that authorises the process, if required. The role may need to have a particular skill set, be professionally qualified, or have a certain level of security clearance to carry out the activities.

At a certain level of detail of a process diagram, the 'WHO' may be a department rather than a role. This is more common in the creation of the 'To Be' solution, because at the time a solution is being created it may be easier to establish which department will 'own' a part of the process and what the dependencies and deliverables will be before it is agreed which roles within that department will carry out the activities. One reason for this could be the role may end up being a new one.

Also include the number of people carrying out the role. This can be very useful in diagnostics and analysis.

For example, if a department has 50 staff feeding 300 orders per week into an application, and the next department in the process only has 15 staff that can only deal with a maximum of 120 orders per week, then it should not be a surprise that there is a bottleneck or constraint in the second department.

WHAT: This is the list of activities included within the process, the communications between the roles, the purpose of the process, what there is to achieve, and the business rules associated with the process. If there are decision points within the process then the rules, how often the rules are reviewed and who by, are included.

Also include the maximum volumes that the roles in the process can deal with. An exception scenario within a process might not be that anything changes in terms of the tasks involved in the scenario, but rather that the volume of items going through the process exceeds the maximum number that can be delivered by the number of people carrying out the roles.

WHERE: This includes the physical locations where the people who carry out the roles are located. It includes the departmental locations if applicable. It also includes the 'where' in the process a particular set of activities would take place in terms of timing.

WHY: This will include the organisation's business goals and strategies and where this process fits into the overall structure. It includes the metrics to report the process. This will be the principal metric that is to be improved.

HOW: This will include applications used, including screenshots and error codes if wrong information is input into the process, systems used, documentation used including the review cycles for the documentation, data used (metadata/taxonomy, etc).

The figure below shows a high level view of an 'Enterprise Architecture'. Whether it is built from the bottom up or the top down, doesn't matter. The important thing is that all the content is collected.

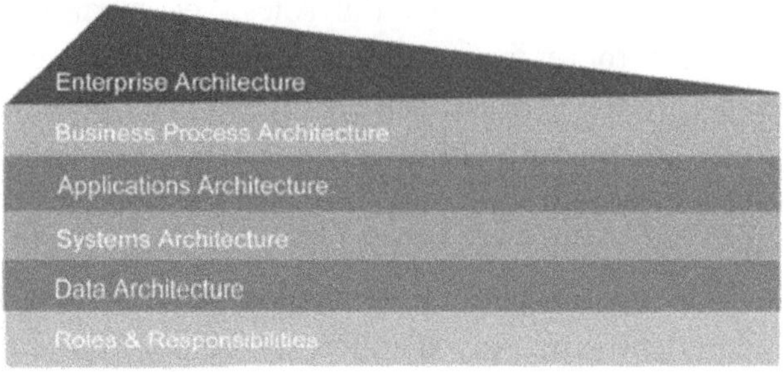

Figure 7 – Enterprise Architecture Model

The Enterprise Architecture is a term used to define the layers of information that should be gathered in building a picture of the organisation so that any and all the areas of potential impact are taken into consideration. Section 9.2 goes into more detail about the Enterprise Architecture content. However, at a high level there are four main types of process:

- Person-to-application processes
- Application-to-applications process
- Application-to-person processes
- Person-to-person processes

Efficiencies are likely to come from automating as much of the application-to-application processes as possible and creating workflow for the other processes.

For our purposes there are five layers to this cake; processes are at the top but they are underpinned by applications. These applications have to run on systems, so they are underpinned by systems. Systems cannot perform without data, so data has to be provided. Lastly the process will need people, so you need to facilitate the people.

The Business Process Components table in Section 13.1 gives you a checklist of things to analyse which will gain you that understanding.

For those that have had training in ITIL (Information Technology Infrastructure Library) Version 2, then the Configuration Management Database (CMDB) should hold the applications, systems, roles, their locations and the interdependencies between them. However, this does not hold processes or process owners. So this information will need to be captured elsewhere. (NB – ITIL Version 3 has redefined a CMDB as a Configuration Management System, as ITSMF has decided that it is not realistic to expect to hold all this information in a single location.)

An understanding of the scenarios and variations which run through a business process, will also need to be established. It is too simplistic to believe that 'everything' can be mapped and analysed. Unless an organisation has inexhaustible resources, then this phase needs to be targeted.

The 'Pareto Principle', or 80/20 rule, should be employed here, as eighty per cent of the volume of activity that goes through a process will go through twenty per cent of the scenarios, or perhaps even less. Therefore initial analysis should lead to the highest volume path through a process.

Alternatively, if this information is not available initially, the first scenario should be the most straightforward scenario through the process. This is sometimes referred to as a 'happy path' or 'golden path' and can be defined as a scenario where the answer to any question/gateway is 'Yes', so the business analyst will have a spine of a process from start to finish. Additional scenarios can be added by going to the first question and following the scenario if the answer to that question had been 'No'.

Variations are defined as something different but in the same scenario, for example an increase in volume, or the same scenario being triggered by a different role or external process, and so on.

In time a fuller process model can be built, but initially I'd recommend one that holds only business critical processes with the highest volume scenarios.

The Object Management Group defines process modelling as:

> 'The capturing of an ordered sequence of business activities and supporting information that describe how a business pursues its objectives.'

There are many process mapping tools on the market and the level of complexity you need to map will dictate the level of detail you will capture. The amount of investment you plan to spend and how 'formal' you want to make the mapping of your processes will all be factors on the application you buy.

You can map simple drawings, which are really no more than electronic versions of large sheets of brown paper and multiple 'Post-it' notes. The 'Post-it' form of capture is a very cheap and fast method to capture process, and the basic modelling notation (see section 9.3) can still be used. You will still need to transfer this information into some form of application so it can be stored and circulated for approval, and there are many mapping tools on the market.

A simple process map is one where there is not a great deal of detail, but where the basic flow of activities is captured.

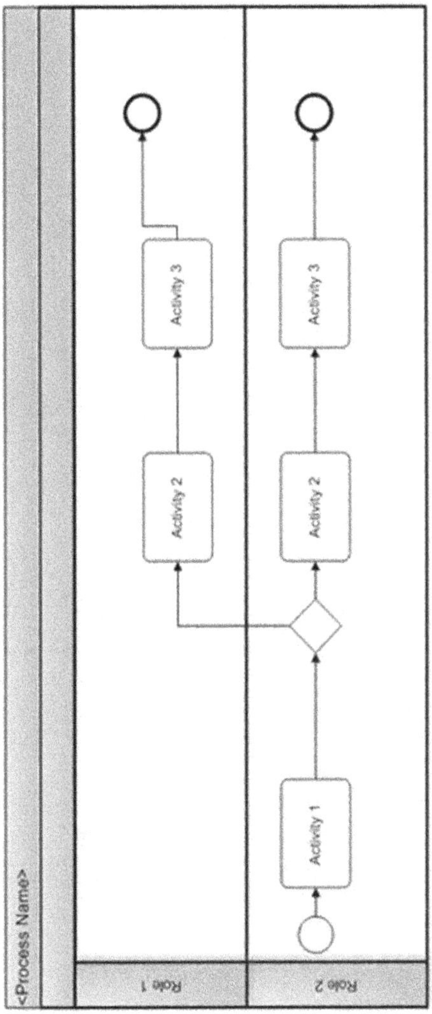

Figure 8 – Simple Process Map

The map above was created using Microsoft Visio. It includes the roles involved, the start and end points, a gateway that represents a decision point and the activities carried out.

This will be a pictorial representation of the roll of paper and Post-it representation of a process.

Still within Visio or other applications, more complex process diagrams can be drawn.

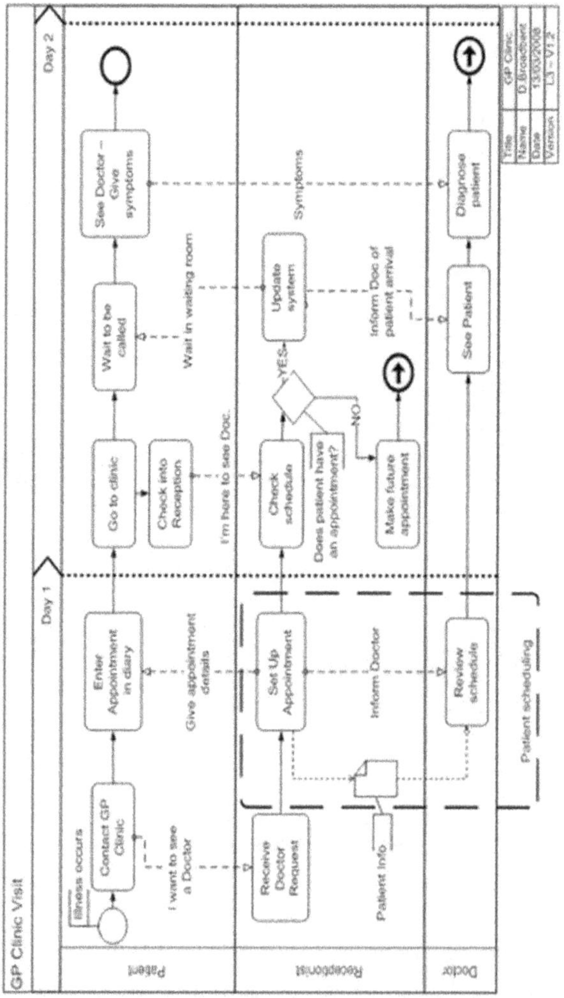

Figure 9 - Process Map with attachments

The figure above is still a simple process map, but it has more information than the previous simple map. This has defined roles, it has the messages that pass between the roles, it has attachments, it is under version control and it has business governance for the decisions to be made. Yet it is still described as a simple process because tools like Visio won't do simulations of process. If a multi-layered process has been drawn and something is changed at a high level, it is not automatically changed at lower levels.

Therefore, as these maps become more complex, it also becomes more difficult to ensure that they maintain their accuracy. Because if process maps are not kept up-to-date and used as the backbone of formal change management, there is the risk that the whole programme creates some very graphic pictures for the walls of the office, but with little real value.

However, equally I would not advocate plunging into buying a hugely expensive process mapping application, unless you are going to use over 90% of its capability. Having a tool that can run simulations is only an advantage if you have the accurate information to populate them. There are process mining tools that can assist in the population of such tools, but again these need data.

So, what should be mapped? The answer is that an organisation should have a good understanding of its critical business processes. This will be investigated in Section 8.

7.4 Solution Creation

Once the goals have been set and the 'As Is' has been mapped and verified, then the work can begin to see what needs to be done to bridge the gap between where an organisation 'is' and 'where it's trying to get to'.

The creation of this 'solution' should be carried out by the team that is going to be carrying out the work and who carried the first two stages of the approach. This is a key point because to ensure 'ownership' of the solution, the team that will implement it needs to be part of its creation. This can also be an important step in tackling some of the resistance to change. If the change is created and communicated from within a team, it will not be seen as being 'imposed' upon the team. Resistance can come from people feeling that change had been imposed upon them from senior managers.

The Enterprise Architecture Components list (Section 13.1) the various aspects of an organisation that can be affected by change. Therefore, this is the list that will need to be verified in the creation of the solution. The solution may have aspects from all the layers of: Process, Applications, Systems, Data, Data Objects and Roles.

7.4.1 Stage 1 Solution Creation

Hold a workshop that has on the walls the 'As Is' and 'To Be' process maps and decide in terms of 'components' what will need to change between one and the other. This will start to form the business requirements.

List your requirements in terms of:

- Must have
- Could have
- Won't have

An 'Assumptions register' will need to be filled in while this workshop is being run to enable its completion. The verification of these assumptions will obviously need to take place before the solution is implemented.

7.4.2 Change Products

The solution will have a number of deliverable 'Change Products'. Some products may be simple and some will be complex.

A simple product can be anything: a new form, the agreement to add people to a distribution list, a report, a piece of software, anything that the change team will deliver to the organisation, but it doesn't have to be delivered in a 'waterfall' method of lots of planning due to the complexity of the requirements, but not deliverable for a substantial length of time.

I deliberately avoid the term 'quick wins' because sometimes there can be the assumption by senior management that there will be instant benefit and quick wins. This is communicated to the organisation and an unrealistic expectation is set, particularly if it turns out that this is not the case. This will additionally do more damage as it can give the programme a bad press initially before it's even got off the ground. On the other hand, if you do not set false expectations and then something is discovered that can be delivered early as a product, then the programme gets a boost, some positive press and those involved get a boost as they can see the fruits of their labour very early on. It is also ammunition to throw at the ones who expressed the negative, 'we've seen all this before, it will never work because the others haven't' sort of attitude. Even if these people themselves are not convinced, it will have an effect on those around them that they are trying to influence. So I would always recommend that terms like 'quick wins' are not used unless you can articulate them and deliver them.

Even before the 'As is' and 'To Be' drawings have been completed, there may have been things that just spring out as dysfunctional parts of the current process which could be remedied with something simple. For example, three parts of the end-to-end process use three separate forms for the activities they carry out, but each department contacts the customer to get the same minimum data set (name, address, telephone numbers, email, etc) to populate their form. A product could be a new form that captures all the information that all three departments use, but collects it only once from the customer and then all three departments share the information. This could be one of the 'pains' referred to earlier.

Some products will be more complex and will be approached as either mini-projects or full blown projects in their own right, depending on the complexity, but they will all fall under the umbrella of the 'Change Programme Implementation Plan'. To avoid misunderstanding, the term 'project' will refer to products delivered within the change programme so the journey should not be referred to as a change project, because projects end and continual improvement does not end.

Where this approach differs from others you may have come across before is in how the gaps are bridged and constraints and duplications removed by the use of change products, and how these products are communicated to the people in the organisation. There will be regular communications to all staff. There will also be targeted communications to specific groups who will directly benefit from particular change products – see below.

In this way, staff will know – at all times – what changes are coming and the staff will be in a better position to understand how these change products will affect them.

To summarise, a product is anything that:

- Impacts the current performance of the process.
- Requires members of the team to carry out tasks to achieve the delivery of the product.

One of the advantages of this approach is that products can be delivered in an 'Agile' method of continual improvement, where a number of versions of the product can be quickly delivered. Each version gives the organisation something more than the previous version, but the organisation does not have to wait for the final version before gaining any benefit. To continue the example above, the first product might simply be an agreed distribution list of names in departments two and three, who require the minimum data set that department one have already collected from the customer, and the agreement that from a particular date department one will collect the data as they currently did in any case, but will additionally will send a copy of the form to the distribution list. Departments two and three will strip out the minimum data set and therefore will not need to bother the customer.

The second version of the product might encompass a form that is filled in by department one that includes the data above the minimum data set which departments two and three require, so the customer is contacted only once and a single version of the truth is used all the way through the process.

The third version of the product might be the on-line version of the form that the customer fills in themselves, ensuring all the information has been spelled correctly because the customer has done it themselves.

The fourth version of the form is an on-line form that only asks the customer for certain information depending on the scenario they are following in the process, thereby not asking for any information that is not going to be used.

The customers will already know this process is poor because they are being contacted on multiple occasions for what to them is the same information, so they would notice an instant improvement.

Each version is better than the one before, so the product is replaced by the better product, but the organisation doesn't have to wait until the web form has been developed and implemented before any improvement to the process is made.

- Product A, version 1 – A distribution list and an agreement to send forms to it.
- Product A, version 2 – An extended form that replaces all three forms by containing all the data required by all three departments.
- Product A, version 3 – An on-line form that the customer can fill in themselves.
- Product A, version 4 – An on-line form with intelligence built in, based on process scenarios, so only collects the data pertaining to what the customer requires.

In the short term when version 2 is being used, the first department might need additional resource as they are capturing all the data and this resource might be supplied by departments two and three. The web form will take time to develop, test and implement, but each product has made the process more efficient and the organisation and customers didn't have to wait until version 4 before any benefit was delivered.

The development of product will roughly follow the following stages:

- Define product
- Define the tasks to create, test and implement the product
- Agree resource
- Agree timescales
- Agree funding (if required)
- Get sign-off from programme sponsor
- Deliver

NB. Delivery can be by either a Strategic (Sec 7.5) or Tactical (Sec 7.6) approach.

Some products will be delivered in-house and some may require the use of partners or external suppliers, which may require invitations to tenders and so on, but they will all be run under the umbrella of the change programme. The statements of requirements and project initiation documents will include the references to the processes they will impact and how, so this can also be communicated to the organisation.

In this way realistic expectations can be set for the organisation. Progress will be communicated to the staff so people will know what the change programme is doing, where the change programme is up to, and staff will see the change programme delivering tangible benefits to the organisation.

In a similar way to the ITIL definition of the various types of change, I have adopted four levels of change product:

- Standard Change Product
- Minor Change Product
- Significant Change Product
- Major Change Product

7.4.2.1 Standard Change Product

This category is for low risk, pre-approved change products. They are common and follow a set procedure. A request for change would be logged, but it would be fast-tracked as it would not require authorisation. All of these change products would be in a Service Catalogue which the change team would publish to the organisation.

For example, a person leaves the company and a new person takes over the role. The new person is now the owner of a number of end-to-end processes, or is the owner of a form. This change would update the Business Operations Model with the new person's details. There are no changes to the processes or to the forms themselves.

7.4.2.2 Minor Change Product

This category is for change products that will impact the organisation but not greatly. It might be that this is the first version of a change product. Versions will be discussed in more detail later, but this means that an agile approach is used to get quick change products implemented with the minimum of fuss. See Tactical Business Improvement Section 7.6.

An example might be that finance decides to split into two, covering corporate capital expenditure finance and operational day-to-day expenditure finance. Therefore, the processes that include finance would need to be reviewed so the right finance sub-department is on the process map.

The Change Manager will be able to sign off a minor change product under his or her own authority.

7.4.2.3 Significant Change Product

This category is for changes that either require a large amount of resource for a short time to implement a particular change product, or require a resource for a significant length of time that they would not be doing their day job, but there is sufficient benefit to the business that it is deemed sufficiently important that it can't wait.

These levels of change product will need to go via a Change Advisory Board (CAB). The make-up of the CAB will vary depending on the change products, but will usually include a number of senior managers including operations, IT and finance. They will ascertain the return on investment, the risks, the resources required and will appoint a change (Project) manager who will be responsible for the implementation.

7.4.2.4 Major Change Product

This category covers change products which are sufficiently complex that they are projects in their own right. They will be set up as standard Prince2 projects and the CAB will usually be the steering committee for the project. This will usually include members from the steering committee for the full change programme.

An example might be that, as part of a change programme, an organisation is going to replace the IT call management application.

7.4.3 Requirements

Solution developers will often ask organisations for their functional and non-functional specifications so they can translate these into technical specifications and see if their current product range can tick all the 'must haves' within its standard (vanilla flavour) configuration, or how much work it will take to be able to tick all the boxes. If the work will be likely to increase the cost significantly, then the applications' provider may decide not to respond to the 'invitation to tender'.

I would advise organisations to first create a document that lays out what their 'Business Requirements' are. What do you want your 'solution' to be able to achieve in business terms? This will be based upon the metric you are trying to improve. This will set the scene for those organisations that will respond to your invitation to tender in terms that the solutions have to be more than simply IT-based.

Too often organisations make the mistake of believing that the only aspect that needs to be investigated is the IT aspect, in terms of software and hardware. Terms like 'functional' and 'non-functional' do not cover process or cultural aspects of the cycle. 'Functional' covers the things the new application is meant to be able to 'do'. Non-functional covers things like system security, response times to key strokes, disaster recovery requirements, etc.

On occasions non-functional requirements may include some more subjective requirements, for example, 'the new solution must be easy to use'. It may be difficult to design a metric to measure 'easy to use' as some people might pick up using the solution very fast while others may struggle. So if these kinds of subjective measures are to be used, they still need to have metrics. 'Easy to use' can be translated into 'a person should be able to use the solution without assistance within 30 minutes', now you have a non-functional requirement that is at least measurable.

The 'As is' analysis will have flagged up the constraints, gaps and duplications in the current process.

7.4.4 Stage 2 Solution Creation

The above workshops will have created the output that can be put into a document that states what it is the organisation is trying to achieve. It will have established where certain pieces of data will be held and which roles in the organisation will 'own' the integrity of the data if it is to be shared by other parts of the end-to-end process.

Often these workshops will run for a number of days, as issues will get raised and decisions will need to be taken as to whether a certain aspect will be included within this programme or it is sufficiently being covered in another programme that it can be stated as 'out of scope' for this programme.

The next stage is to break this solution down into manageable deliverables that are seen as 'achievable' in terms of their requirements of resource, time and cost. To achieve this you will use 'change products' – see above.

7.4.5 Stage 3 – Business Impact Assessments

One of the key stages that has to be carried out before a new solution can be implemented is a business impact assessment. This will establish what the impact on the business will be of implementing the new solution.

The analysis of the gap between where you start from and where you are trying to get to, will basically build your project plan for the various things that will need to take place to get you to your target. However, once you have identified the gaps and what needs to take place, you also need to look at the impact of making those changes, both in cultural terms as well as impacts on things like systems and processes.

As mentioned earlier you will need to establish the lenses through which you will look to fully understand the impact that the changes will make.

The impact on:

- Business processes (including timings)
- Applications (licences, etc)
- Systems (hosting limitations, etc)
- Roles and responsibilities (for individuals and departments)
- Business objects (including print cycles of forms if you have external forms printed)
- Data (both Static and Dynamic – Static where is it fixed so calculations can be carried out on it, and Dynamic – where it's being constantly updated)

Often projects are not given the time to properly carry out business impact assessments. An element of 'due diligence' is usually included in project plans, but rarely is it sufficient to really talk to people and thereby gain an understanding of the 'impact' of implementing the project. It is worth bearing in mind that even organisations which are very good at communicating to their staff still struggle to stay ahead of the 'rumour mill'.

The thing you don't really want during any project is surprises; as mentioned earlier, the unknown unknowns. So the better the impact analysis, the better the project, and the less likely that surprises will occur because surprises usually cost money and time.

So to look at these in slightly more detail, what would be the impact on these business areas?

Business process:

- Process Governance
  - Business rules; how will the process display the new business rules associated with the process, so that people will know how to use the process?
  - What are the process defaults? Are they different from 'As Is'?
  - How are the defaults displayed?
  - Service Level Agreements – how will the SLA thresholds be set, triggered, escalated and reported?
  - Operational Level Agreements – how will the OLA thresholds be set, triggered, escalated and reported?
  - What will the exception process flows be?
- Process timings (how will they be captured and measured?)
  - Sequential timings
  - Cumulative timings
- Interdependencies
  - Role definitions
  - Locations/departments
  - External parties

  - External systems/applications
  - Approval thresholds
- Functional requirements
  - Functional flows (role-to-role via a scenario-based process)
  - Menu security/authorisation thresholds
  - Testing – is the process part of a minimum process test set used when anything gets changed?

The impact of changing the business process may affect any or all of the above. Just for clarification, a Service Level Agreement (SLA) is a contractual agreement between a company and an external company, whether they are a supplier or a customer, which lays out certain tasks which will be delivered within an agreed timescale, to a certain level of quality and with escalation routes on both sides should the service not be delivered. Sometimes these agreements include financial penalties for non-conformance.

An Operational Level Agreement (OLA) is similar to an SLA in that it is an agreement that things will be done to an agreed level of quality within an agreed timescale, however, an OLA is within an organisation, usually between departments, and is to ensure that a cross-functional end-to-end process runs efficiently. Each of the senior managers responsible for operational areas involved in the process sign up to the OLA. The construction of an OLA may be controversial within your organisation because the organisational 'owners' will be expected to sign up to the OLA and be willing to be measured on their department's ability to deliver to that OLA.

As I have already mentioned, the manner in which you re-engineer a process will be in direct relation to the metrics you are trying to improve. So process timings may well be something you expect the project to have an impact on, and may well be a measurement of the success of the project.

Interdependencies are always important, the impact assessment will establish what people currently do in the context of the process that is about to change. Many organisations use business process re-engineering projects to reduce headcount. But the impact assessment may uncover that a post you might think of cutting is actually vital to other processes working end-to-end, or the process you are looking to improve may actually be 10%-20% of that full time employee's work.

- Applications
    - Licences: New applications may well require the purchasing of new licences, these might have 'User' licences and 'Administrator' licences. Usually administrator licences are significantly more expensive than an average user licence, so you will need to think how many of these types of licences you will need.
    - Existing applications: existing applications that are being used might have long term or lifetime licences and if the application is being replaced, then the removal of the old application may need to be part of the project plan. Existing applications may also be being used by other parts of the organisation for other pieces of work, so analysis of all who use an application is important during BIA so as not to do any harm to the day-to-day operations of the business when the application is turned off.
    - Local solutions: There might be local applications that have been bought to do the process you are re-engineering. In some cases your project might be seen as going back in time, if the current local gives them everything they think they need and your new application doesn't.
- Systems
    - Servers
    - Networks
    - Peripherals

All of the above may need to be upgraded or replaced. These days there is always the option for 'Cloud' computing, where you use an external organisation to provide the space you need to run all your business process calculations, but the hosting is their problem and really all you need is an internet connection. Either way, an assessment of the current hardware will need to take place.

- Roles and Responsibilities
  - Core skills required to carry out the new process (so that an assessment of the current skills can be assessed)
  - Organisational role(s) that will carry out the tasks
  - Security profile/threshold

All existing roles will need to be understood in the context of the process you are changing. Organisations that are spread across a country, or are spread across multiple countries, may use people from different departments to operate the existing process, so the understanding of 'who' will own the process going forward and how this will impact current roles is key to business impact assessments.

- Object Management (Source – Output, how will it differ from 'As is' to 'To be')
  - Where does the data come from?
  - Where does it go to?
  - What business role 'owns' the object?
  - What is its review cycle?
  - Object examples:
    - Paper documents, forms, drop-down lists, electronic forms, SMS messages, voicemails, IVR instructions and prompts, reports, databases, spreadsheets, emails, etc.
- Data
  - Taxonomy used
  - Metadata tags used

  - Data Dictionary
  - Links

In the business impact assessment, the current data used should be the same data used going forwards. There may be a need to identify where certain data is collected and why certain data is not passed onto other departments. In the case study later in this book you will see the impact of what happens when one department has the ability to collect data but either doesn't collect it, or collects it but doesn't pass it on to those departments that need it. Some processes need to lock down data for the purposes of the process, e.g. to calculate commission, this data becomes static and does not change, whereas other data, e.g. performance data for reporting, will continually be collected. This is dynamic data.

- Reporting
  - How is the process currently measured/reported, when it works ok?
  - How is the process currently measured/reported when it does not work ok?
  - When it does not work well, the escalation goes:
    - To whom – to what role?
    - At what frequency?
    - Are there report consolidation levels where they get 'rolled up' for senior management?
    - Is an OLA in place?

Existing reporting should be investigated as part of impact assessments. A good understanding of how the business currently analyses what it does, to ensure that certain reporting (financial, audit, e.g. Sarbanes Oxley) can still be carried out. The reporting may be general reports where all the information is pulled into a data cube so it can be cut and sliced by business analysts. It may be analytical reports, which reports the top 5% and bottom 5%, so that lessons can be learned. And, there can be any number of exception reports generated, e.g. when a service level or operational level agreement has been breached.

A great deal of time is used up within organisations to generate reports. From a business process re-engineering perspective, it is always a good idea to analyse whether all the reports currently being generated are of value. A good benchmark of value is whether any business decisions are made as a result of a report, or which reports lead to business decisions being made. Because if no business decisions are being made on the back of a report being generated, you should question the value of that report.

This list is not exhaustive by any means. The business needs to get to a place of comfort that enables them to be convinced that the solution is 'fit for purpose'. The level of business impact assessment enquiries will be driven by the amount of risk it is believed the implementation may cause.

7.4.6 Stage 4 – Communications Plan

In the preparation stage, the initial communications plan will be kicked off by the senior management to articulate their buy-in and 'set the scene' for the organisation. At that stage the methods of ongoing communication will be discussed.

It will demonstrate the importance of this programme in the context of any other project or programme being delivered at the same time.

It will send out a number of messages:

- It will demonstrate the level of 'Buy-in' from senior management.
- It will let all staff that might have fallen into the category of Refusal in 'Resistance to change' know the importance of

this project. See 'Resistance to Change' section 11.2 in part two of this book. These individuals may not wish to assist in the delivery of the project, but they will often not wish to be labelled as someone who got in its way or was disruptive in any way. This alone may get the people working on the project through a number of otherwise closed doors.
- It will give the project team a tangible mandate that can be used if 'scope creep' begins, even on occasions needing that mandate to wave in front of the senior management who agreed it in the first place.

Initially it may have no more than the aspirations of the programme, but it will have the schedule of communication, so it will set expectations to the staff of when they will hear the next instalment of what is happening. As the project gets closer to the stage of having the 'solution' signed off and the implementation plan agreed, then more communications will be able to let staff know what is happening in more detail.

These updates are usually written by the team delivering the project and top and tailed by the senior management sponsor.

Once the team gets to the solutions creation stage, the products that will be delivered can be communicated to the organisation. When they are delivered, their benefit can be communicated to the organisation. This will enable the change programme to always be current and seen to be delivering tangible benefits to the organisation, rather than some nebulous project going on somewhere else behind closed doors that the management said was important a while ago.

I would recommend something at least monthly that would include:

- Products' previous forecast to be delivered within this month
- Updates on those products

- Products' forecast to be delivered in the following month
- Timescales for product release or updated versions of products
- Updates on progress of complex products

The communications plan will be tailored to your individual organisation but its primary purpose is to ensure that resistance to the programme does not emerge within the organisation. One of the most common reasons people have been known to develop resistance to change is that they feel they were never communicated with when the change programme began. Therefore, it is imperative that what is being done is known to the people in the organisation that it will affect. A 'No Surprises' policy is a good one and a continuous communications plan will ensure everyone knows what is happening.

The case study described later in this book has a number of options that can be used in the 'Selling' of a communication plan to the staff of an organisation. However, the most important aspect is that the person who delivers the message is the 'Subject Matter Expert' who came from that area of the business initially. This is very important, because hearing a message from one of their own teammates will give the message a level of credibility it can never have if delivered by a senior manager or an external consultant.

7.5 Strategic Solutions Implementation

Once the 'solution' has been created, then it can be implemented. As described in the previous section, the implementation will depend on the product being implemented. Some of the implementations will be seen as tactical and some will be seen as strategic in nature.

Tactical implementations will be described in section 7.6 and will include agile methods of delivery. Strategic implementations can best be defined as products, or a series of linked products, that are sufficiently complex that they warrant a project approach in their own right.

7.5.1 Managing Strategic implementations (Complex Change Products)

I would advocate the use of industry standard methodologies to implement your solution, such as PRINCE2. However, I have come across a number of successful projects that have been implemented using cut-down versions of PRINCE that called themselves P.I.N.O. – 'Prince in name only'.

Communication is very important at this stage. The organisation needs to fully understand the difference between a 'programme' and a 'project'. A project should have a defined start and a defined end. A change management programme is a cycle of continual improvement, therefore it should never end. However, the programme can include a number of projects as well as other products. The only way a programme should be 'concluded' is when the practices employed are so well known within an organisation's culture that continual improvement is the 'norm', and therefore having it as a defined programme is no longer required.

As mentioned, a product might be something as simple as a new form that replaces three previous existing forms. For more complex products, deliver them as mini-projects with defined tasks for each person.

Ensure each task is checked so that the person carrying out that task is given the time to establish his or her dependencies to achieve the task and the realistic time they forecast the task will take if they are provided with all of these dependencies. Once this has happened, the Project Manager can carry out project reviews that will focus on the tasks in terms of 'days from completion' instead of 'percentage completed'.

Too often I have seen tasks on project plans get to the '80% complete' stage and stay there for weeks or months because a dependency to be able to complete the task has not been achieved.

Implementation of any project also needs to be set in the context of other projects that aim to go-live at the same time. Organisations implement multiple projects simultaneously and often there are only minor teething problems that need to be sorted out. However, sometimes large problems emerge because more than one project has tried to change the same process but in different ways. Both projects may require the same new application and, as a result, may also require additional disk storage space on shared drives. Initial acceptance testing may not show up the fact that both projects are attempting to change the same process but in different ways.

7.5.2 Testing solutions prior to implementation

Unless the organisation is using a test management application or has mapped a business process model, it may be difficult to ascertain whether more than one project will adversely affect a process until it is too late. I believe it is reasonable to ask any IT department how it currently ensures that the same process is not being adversely affected by more than one project.

Comprehensive testing should be carried out on any complex products that are to be delivered. Although there are many testing regimes and types of testing, the main requirement is to reach a point where the introduction of the product has been tested to such an extent that its introduction into the live environment is an acceptable risk.

Section 13.2 looks at this in greater detail however the fundamentals are that firstly the requirements are established and these should have:

- Quantifiable requirements. Each requirement should be specific and measurable. Therefore each requirement will have a quantifiable metric that allows the test manager to establish whether the test outcome meets the requirement or not.
- Coherency and Consistency. The project specification will contain a definition of the meaning of every essential subject matter term within the specification. Does it? Is every reference to a defined term consistent with its definition?
- Context. Set the context for the project. The context defines:
    - The problem that the organisations are trying to solve.
    - It contains all the requirements that the organisations must eventually meet.
    - It contains anything that the organisations have to build
    - It contains anything the organisations have to change.
- Completeness. Completeness is to question whether the organisations have captured all the requirements that are currently known, or whether the requirements have been written from only one point of view.

Once the requirements have been established, the business process should be established and the scenarios within them that will form part of the test schedule, sometimes referred to as Test Cases within 'Blackbox Testing'.

Many organisations will already have established a minimum test pack used for the testing of all new applications and systems. If this is the case it should be used, if not a test pack based on the critical business processes should be created, so that all products can be shown as passing a basic criteria before they are implemented.

7.5.3 Operational Proving

In certain circumstances it may be possible to carry out operational proving as part of the test cycle. Operational proving is where the new process is actually followed using the new applications, systems, data and roles to carry it out, only on a much smaller scale than the actual go-live will be. When standard UAT is carried out, a number of business scenarios may be followed in a test cell environment with machines not on the formal network but in a test cell environment.

Operational proving will use the new application for real. For example, one retail organisation was migrating a large number of customers from a number of old applications onto a new single application at the same time as a new website was being launched. The operational proving team set up a number of real accounts in the new application and gave a number of volunteers actual money in these accounts and got them to shop. The items were ordered on the new website that the public did not have access to, but the orders flowed through into the warehouse management system and were tracked to ensure the goods turned up at people's front doors. Then the items were returned and the return cycle tracked the items back into the warehouse and the accounts were credited with the money.

This exercise threw up a number of anomalies that would not have been found in the standard user acceptance testing. For example, the GPS application being used by the delivery part of the organisation to locate the customers' premises used postcodes. It became apparent that if customers lived in either apartments or flats which shared a postcode, the current system would not hold a flat or apartment number in addition to the overall building address that was associated with the postcode. This was rectified and re-tested before go live.

Operational Proving gives an organisation the opportunity to iron out the 'teething problems' before go-live, and therefore not have to sort them out in view of customers. If organisations believe that this is an expensive overspend, I would recommend they read the number of case studies that will be written about the problems British Airways had at the opening of Terminal Five at Heathrow Airport in the United Kingdom in 2008.

7.5.4 Post Go-Live

Once the project has gone live, it is common practice to hold a post project review. This review is generally asking 'what would you do differently knowing what you know now?'

Numerous reports and surveys have been published over the years when Project Managers have been interviewed about what the common findings are in post project reviews. The most common answer is that more planning should have been done.

Where this review will add real value is that it will establish the lessons learned so that mistakes are not repeated the next time the cycle is run, because this is a continuous cycle.

7.6 Tactical Business Improvement

7.6.1 Implement Tactical Change

During the workshop to establish the initial areas of 'pain', a number of simple products may have been defined (see above). There may also be occasions when analysis carried out after mapping the initial scenarios of the critical business processes discovers something that can be implemented quickly. These easier 'products' can be introduced quickly, but should still be introduced in a structured manner. The introduction of these products should be owned and managed by the change management function or programme office.

This fits neatly into standards for change such as ITIL, as these would be changes that fit in the categories of standard, minor or significant.

7.6.2 Introduction of the Eight Stage Tactical Business Improvement Process

This can be introduced in parallel to the Strategic Plan and can be up and running in a very short space of time. This will allow simple or easier products to be delivered in a short space of time.

Ideas will arise through an operational incident being raised within the organisation, a problem arising within the organisation, a strategic change in direction, a forum suggestion or business analysis of a particular process. When an idea arises it needs to be raised as a 'tactical change product', logged into a database or some sort of log to audit the ideas; who suggested the idea so credit can be given, when, why, forecast benefits, etc. It can then be defined in terms of a deliverable product to the organisation.

As previously mentioned, an 'Agile' approach can be adopted which will allow a number of versions of a product. Although there are eight gates a product will need to go through to get delivered, there is nothing stopping it getting through a number of gates in a single meeting. This allows rapid development and delivery of products.

7.6.2.1 1st Gate – Definition

First gate is definition of product – The product will be assessed in relation to the overall metric that is trying to be improved. If the product does not align with this, then the questions should be asked as to why the product should be delivered. There may be good business reasons why a product might be considered, even if it is not necessarily part of the change programme as such, but it is established that it will benefit the organisation.

There might be a good reason why a product does not get beyond this stage initially. But it would remain on the database.

7.6.2.2 2nd Gate – Alignment

Second gate is alignment – The product is reviewed in terms of its relation to other products or versions of products, to agree the schedule of implementation.

The product would also be reviewed at Level 2/3 to ascertain what processes would be affected by the delivery of this product to ensure that its introduction does not adversely affect a process.

7.6.2.3 3rd Gate – Tasks

Third gate is definition of tasks – This stage looks at what has to be done to create, test and implement the product. As this stage it might be decided that the product will be delivered to the organisation in a series of versions. In this way the time taken to deliver an earlier version might be much quicker, it might not have all the final features of the product but adds sufficient benefit to the organisation that it warrants being created.

To enable rapid testing it is recommended that a 'minimum test pack' is created based on critical business processes, scenarios and volumes.

7.6.2.4 4th Gate – Resource

Fourth Gate is resource – Agree who in the team will carry out the creation, testing and implementation.

At this stage if any funding is required, it will be established.

7.6.2.5 5th Gate – Timescales

Fifth Gate is Timescales – Agree what is the delivery timescale, based on the tasks that have to be undertaken and other workload being carried out by the resource. Both the sequential and cumulative timescales should be established.

7.6.2.6 6th Gate – Sign Off

Sixth Gate is Sign-off – All products need to be signed off before going into production. The level of sign off and signatories will be decided in the preparation phase of the programme.

The level of sign off may well be on a sliding scale based on a number of factors, any funding requirements, the amount of resource required and the size of the product and so on. The level of sign off should be established at definition stage.

I would recommend that a 'Threshold Approval Process' should be adopted. A threshold approval process establishes a series of financial level of approvals for a series of management positions up to the board of directors.

In this way a resource will be allocated the role of 'Product Manager'. This is in effect the Project Manager for this particular product. They may be the only person working to create this product, or they may lead a number of people to co-ordinate and ensure that the tasks are completed to create the product. They also take on the role of 'Budget Holder'. This role is allowed to allocate a sum of money agreed in the change programme's budget for 'low risk' implementation of products.

This can be signed off by the budget holder and a level 1 signatory. The table below is an example of such a table of funding levels and signatories, however, the principle is that there are only ever two people signing off a product. In this way the introduction of products does not get tied up in a length escalated sign off process.

From	To	Level of Sign off
£1.00	£5,000.00	Budget Holder and Manager
£5001.00	£10,000.00	Budget Holder and Level 1 Signatory
£10,001.00	£20,000.00	Budget Holder and Senior Level 1 Signatory
£20,001.00	£30,000.00	Budget Holder and Level 2 Signatory
£30,001.00	£40,000.00	Budget Holder and Senior Level 2 Signatory
£40,001.00	£50,000.00	Budget Holder and Level 3 Signatory
£50,001.00	£100,000.00	Budget Holder and Senior Level 3 Signatory
£100,001.00	£200,000.00	Change Advisory Board
£200,001.00	£500,000.00	Managing Director
£500K+		Board of Directors

7.6.2.7 7th Gate – Communication

Seventh Gate is communication – All products that are to be delivered to the organisation should be part of a regular communication. If this is a monthly communication, then the products forecast to be delivered in the following month can be described in the communication. Additionally, updates on previously delivered products can be part of the communications plan.

7.6.2.8 8th Gate – Delivery

Eighth Gate is delivery – The tasks are carried out and the product is delivered. The impact of the delivery of the product should be monitored. For products that will have a number of versions, this will be important to ascertain whether the additional benefits were noticed when the latest version of the product was released.

Feedback should be sought for one-off products. If this feedback is positive, then this information should be communicated as part of the regular communications plan, to give the change programme some 'good press'. If the feedback is negative, then the product can be reviewed.

This is important because the change team '**will make mistakes**'. Mistakes are part of learning and the team needs to be allowed to make mistakes and to learn from them. The aim should clearly always be that mistakes are not repeated, but the team will need to have the freedom to attempt things and this will mean taking risks. This is the only way to fuel initiative. So when a product does not deliver the impact it was initially believed it would, the team needs to be able to refine the definition process so other products do not 'fail' in the same way.

7.7 Continual Improvement

As stated, the implementation should not be seen as the end of the cycle. If you have managed to stick to your initial scope, then you will have a 'snag list' of a number of things that will need to be looked at that were deemed as 'out of scope'. These things may well be 'business as usual', but were found to be wrong or a very inefficient way of doing things.

Post Go-live, the processes should be continually monitored to ensure that the changes implemented, firstly – deliver the benefits they were meant to, but also, secondly – that other areas of the process will display constraints, gaps and duplications that will start the cycle all over again. Goldratt's 'Theory of Constraints' demonstrates that once a constraint is removed the maximum throughput of any process will naturally move to the next greatest constraint.

One of the benefits of using an agile approach using progressive versions of change products is that the continual improvement can be mapped and communicated. Planning the implementation of versions of products enables the communication that will let staff know that once a constraint has been removed and the throughput moves to the next greatest constraint, the next version of the change product is already in the pipeline. This demonstrates not only the overall benefit the team is delivering to the organisation, but also the team's understanding of the end-to-end process if they can forecast the next constraint before it occurs.

The reason we now should think of this as 'Business Process Management' rather than 'Business Process Change' is that it is imperative that it is **NOT** seen as a 'one-off', but that your organisation's processes should be managed in the same way as its people, money, IT or anything else are managed.

There are numerous examples of organisations that did not 'change' or 'evolve' continually and as a result were casualties of the global recession.

The Critical Business Processes an organisation uses as the spine of its operational processes need to be continually monitored and managed. Of course, to be able to do this efficiently you will need to be able to identify what a critical business process is. The next section will look at Critical Business Processes in more detail and give you an example from the Retail Sector.

8 Critical Business Processes

8.1 Critical Business Processes

The simplest definition of a critical business process is one that an organisation must still be able to carry out, before, during and after any changes are made to it. In simple terms, for a private sector company the ability to take money would automatically be a critical business process.

It would be my recommendation to choose a limited number of processes, four or less initially, as getting accustomed to the routine of mapping, analysis, solutions creation and implementation is something an organisation needs to get used to, depending on where the organisation is on the Business Process Capability Maturity Model. And being too ambitious initially might make an organisation take on more than can realistically be achieved.

8.2 Retail Critical Business Process

To help define a high level critical business process, I will use an example from the world of retail as a case study. This has not significantly changed in many years.

This should also be something that most people can comprehend as undoubtedly almost all of us are touched by the world of retail, whether we like it or not.

8.2.1 Demand Forecast

Without drifting into a sweeping generalisation, it might come as a surprise to some people who read this book that there is

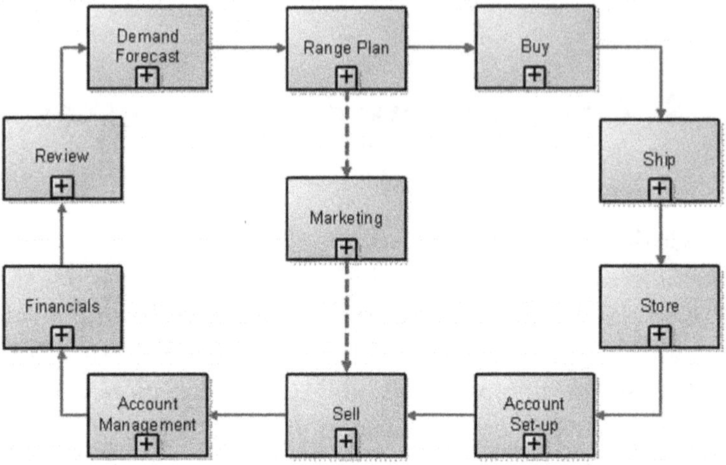

Figure 10 – Critical Business Process – The Retail Lifecycle

more than one 'season' when it comes to fashion, and those people may well be men (speaking as one).

They might not believe that their wardrobe has four seasons of clothes or footwear in it, and they might be right in that belief. However, the women they know will fully understand that there are at least four seasons when it comes to fashion.

And this lifecycle begins with a 'Demand Forecast'. Each retailer has to ask itself the question, 'What are our customers going to want to buy next summer, or winter, etc?' The length of time between the creation of a demand forecast and the final end of the cycle will vary from retailer to retailer.

Some job titles will vary from retailer to retailer, so there is an element of generalisation here. However, in the organisations I have worked with the demand forecast is usually put together by Designers, Buyers and Merchandisers.

Designers and Buyers will go to the fashion shows and see the articles on the catwalks, or they will visit the trade shows and get a 'feel' for what the following season's materials and colours will be for them to make their own designs.

All this information is fed into the demand forecast. And this is fed to the Merchandisers who will create the Range Plan.

8.2.2 Range Plan

Again the job titles may vary, but the distinction between the demand forecast and the range plan is that the buyers and designers may decide the type of items that should be in the forecast and they will also have input into the volumes that get forecast. However, the merchandisers will have the understanding of the types of customer and the demographics of that retailer's customer base.

For example, if the item is a men's shirt then the merchandisers will know that 60% of the men that buy their shirts from that retailer are a $16^1/_2$ inch or size 42 collar, and the make-up of the other 40%, so the amount made or purchased will match the forecast demand. Higher volumes may be sold in 'out of town' outlets than city stores as people might not want to carry as much in city centres. All this information will be used by the retailer to define the range plan.

8.2.3 Buying

Once the types and volumes have been decided, they need to be bought. This will take one of two routes. If an organisation has its own designers, then a number of 'photographic samples' may be made. These are sent to the retailer and put onto models and photographed. Minor adjustments may be made but then a final 'photographic sample' is approved and the items can be manufactured. If an organisation does not have its own designers, then the items will simply be bought following a number of discussions on the colours, materials, size range and so on.

Once these discussions have been concluded, the manufacturing begins and all the processes around contract negotiations will be included in this part of the process.

8.2.4 Shipping

I live in the United Kingdom, and the UK and Europe has a vibrant retail marketplace, however a great deal of the merchandise bought in the UK is not manufactured in either the UK or Europe. A large market for manufacturing exists in the Far East. The quantities manufactured will be large, so there will be a number of processes that will cover the shipping of this stock from its place of manufacture to its place of storage. These will also cover import processes, etc.

In other countries this might not be the case, or the amount of imported goods might not be as high as they are in the UK, but goods will still have to be shipped even if it is only internally within a country, so shipping will still be a factor and part of the critical business process.

8.2.5 Storage

Once the stock is in the country where it will be sold, it will need to be stored. Depending on the selling channel that the retailer employs, namely whether they do most of the selling via internet or through high street shops, will have an impact on the storage of the stock.

Instead of having huge warehouses in shops, many retailers have moved to 'just in time' delivery, where the stock held in the shops is considerably less, the space that had been used as warehouse in the shops becomes 'selling space' and the restocking comes from satellite depots in smaller shipments of items that follow the sales patterns of each shop.

So all these processes that cover the movement of items would be part of this part of the process.

8.2.6 Sell

When the Range Plan is put together, the 'Marketing plan' will also be part of it. How these things will be advertised is thought through very early. Target markets might have different advertising campaigns. Internet, television, cinema, newspapers, catalogues, radio, etc, will all have their own marketing plans.

Some organisations only sell via the internet, therefore saving on expensive shop rental and all the associated costs of running a shop.

Some retailers will 'set up' their customer base, for example, mobile telecommunications companies. So you would need to be a customer to buy their products.

As more and more people use the internet to purchase items, most – if not all – high street shops will also have an internet sales portal.

This part of the process will include 'Sales targets' and it will include the monitoring of sales against forecast. A great deal of work goes into the science of 'volume increase' to 'last buys', so that the retailer has enough stock in when the demand is high and stops manufacturing the item as the interest in the item starts to fall.

8.2.7 Finance

Once the stock has been sold, all the financial information needs to be gathered. Obviously these will be ongoing activities against the forecast, and will interlink with other financial processes.

However, ultimately the organisation will want to know exactly what it sold.

8.2.8 Review

Once an organisation has found out what it finally sold, it can compare this to the original forecast to see whether their customers actually bought what the retailer had forecast their customer was going to buy in the first place.

Lessons will be learned, trend analysis will be updated. Forecast models may be reviewed or changed. Data used to make the initial forecast may be reused if accurate, reviewed and adjusted if not. Jim Womack, the father of the Lean Methodology, once said in a presentation that all forecasts are wrong, some are only a little bit wrong and some are very wrong, but in essence all forecasts are wrong so there will always be a need for some review.

And then the whole process starts again. And in the world of fashion, this will happen at least four times a year. So what usually happens in practice is that all four seasons are continually running, just at different stages of the lifecycle.

Hopefully you will all have been able to follow the logic behind this lifecycle, even if you were not aware of some of the things that took place in it before now. This is important, because if you look at your high street shops and supermarkets and think how much they have changed in the last ten or twenty years – the increase in diversity, the advances of internet portals and so on – yet they still had to maintain all the processes in this lifecycle before, during and after changes were made to them.

9 Process Standards

If I were to take four groups and separately ask them to map a simple process, but didn't give them any standards or scope, I'd expect to get four different maps that would be difficult to interpret if I had not been part of the group that had mapped the process.

PRINCE is an industry standard for managing projects. For many years no such equivalent standard existed for the mapping of business processes.

This section looks at standards which can be used that will ensure that anyone who maps a process will be able to read a map drawn by someone else and vice versa.

9.1 Process Levels

Although there are many organisations that have created applications for the mapping of processes, there is still the issue of interpretation. The level of detail added to maps during the capture of a process is limited to the ability of an organisation to reproduce that map in a way that it can be interpreted with ease.

There are some organisations which maintain that there should be no more than nine boxes on a drawing, or seven plus or minus two. There is nothing wrong with this approach, if your drawings are consistent in their level of detail across an organisation. However, if one part of the organisation is more complex then there can be drill-down after drill-down and, when an analyst is trying to understand an end-to-end process, it can be difficult to follow from one set of maps to another.

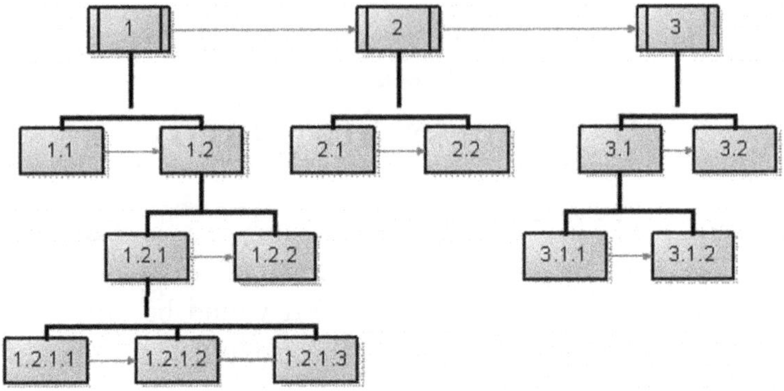

Figure 11 – Process Mapping Drill Down Problem

Those trying to map a business process will often find that one part of a process is more complex than an adjacent part of the process, and as a result have to map it in more detail which means more drill-downs, creating the situation you see above. As you can see, without an understanding of the levels of detail it is difficult to know where you are within a process when trying to follow it. Would you go from 1.2.1.3 to 2.1, or 1.2.2 to 3.1.1? Or would you have to go back up to 1, across to 2 then drill down again?

It is easy to get lost within the structure and not fully understand where you 'are' in the process. But this will lead to problems when you try and re-engineer that drawing, as you won't be able to fully map the impact end-to-end.

There are various schools of thought that state how many levels of detail a drawing should go to. Some look at the levels of detail in terms of whether the drawing is executable, meaning it can be used by a vendor specific tool to automate business processes.

My recommendation is that the levels of detail mapped are consistent across the organisation, so that all those involved in a project understand what they are looking at when they see a drawing.

BPMN is vendor neutral and therefore can be used across a wide range of mapping applications, and BPMN doesn't specify a methodology that should be used.

Therefore this next section is an example of using just four levels of detail, regardless of how many pieces of paper the map ends up on. If your organisational complexity or project requires more levels, then ensure this is fully understood at the start of the project.

- Level 1 – Business Lifecycle Hierarchy
- Level 2 – Operational Departmental Processes
- Level 3 – Role Processes
- Level 4 – Functional Dynamic

Let us look at these in more detail.

9.1.1 Level One – Business Lifecycle/High Level Process

Level one is the highest level view of the process. This can be called the hierarchy of the process, as the end-to-end process can be drilled down from here. This level will explain why the process exists, what its objective is and how it is measured.

This level of process will also have documentation to explain it. How this documentation is attached to the process will vary, depending on the application you have purchased to map and store your organisation's processes.

However, it should contain the following information.

Level 1 – Business Lifecycle Hierarchy
This will include:

- The high level business lifecycle
- Business goals and strategies
- Process Owners

- KPIs and Reporting at Operational/Analytical/ Exception levels

The high level lifecycle will apply to operational processes which are followed on a cycle, for example the retail lifecycle mentioned earlier. If the process is not cyclical, then an explanation of the events that activate it and its forecasted outcomes can be used.

The business goals and strategies of the process will include not only the goals of the process, but also strategies of the organisation and where this process fits into the one, three and five year strategy of the organisation. It is useful that this information be stored in the process documentation as a guide, so that when it is re-engineered those carrying out the work do not lose sight of the overall objectives. Likewise it is an opportunity to challenge if this process is still valid in its current form, if the strategies of an organisation have changed.

Process Owners. Far too few processes are 'owned' in that they have a senior manager who is responsible and accountable for the process end-to-end. An example of this is the New Starter Process.

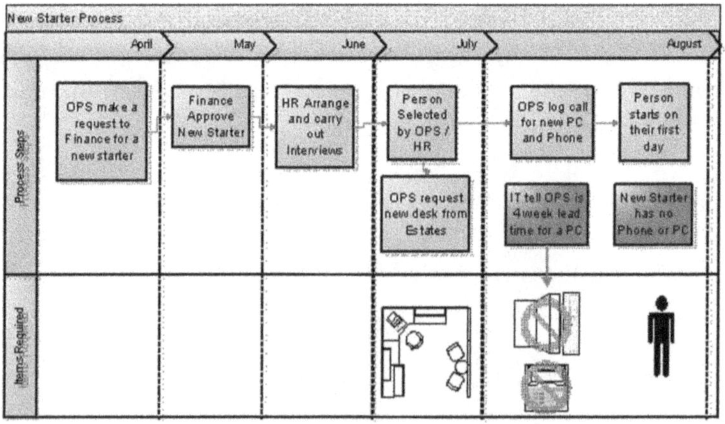

Figure 12 – New Starter Process

In the figure above, you can see that the process involves Operations, Finance, HR, Estates and IT. It is not uncommon that no single senior manager would own the end-to-end process. So although the process started in April, it was August before IT were informed of the new starter coming and then the lead time was four weeks, so the person started their new job with no PC and no telephone. Yet, although the identity of the individual new starter would not be known until after the selection stage in July, the fact that a new starter was going to be joining the company means that IT could have been informed in May. But this didn't happen as Finance, HR and Estates did not see it as their responsibility to tell IT. Operations assumed there would always be lots of PC's and were not aware of the four week lead time that was the Service Level Agreement with the external supplier. The result was that the new starter began working without all the right equipment to carry out their role.

Does this look like your findings from Exercise 1 earlier? Does the new starter process in your organisation have an end-to-end owner? No, I didn't think so.

If a process is 'business critical' then it should be measured. The reports should be at a level where the management can make decisions based upon them. If you are not making decisions based on the output of a report, why are you measuring it? Organisations can fall into the DRIP trap. DRIP = Data – Rich – Information – Poor. If you are getting so many reports that you can't actually digest their meaning and make decisions on them before the next one comes out, then this report is not adding value to your organisation; in fact, it's doing the opposite. At the senior management level the reports that should be reviewed will be Operational, Analytical and Exceptional. Therefore they will cover the overall operational targets. They will cover analytical reports, for example, the top five performing sites and the bottom five performing sites to see what is being done well, so all sites can follow the 'best practices' and what is being done badly, so all sites can avoid doing these things. Exceptional reporting is covering things that are 'one-offs'.

Below is a version of a Level 1 drawing.

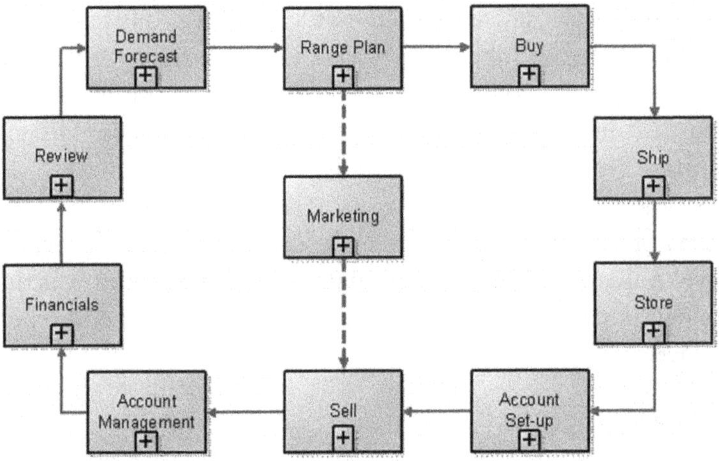

Fig 13– Level 1 Hierarchy/Lifecycle Process Map (Sec8.2)

9.1.2 Level Two – Operational Departmental Processes

Level 2 will include more detail than the high level drawing and will include the departments or stakeholders involved. This will include where the process takes place. In this case the 'where' corresponds to the physical locations of these departments as the locations may have an impact on the performance of a process, and if the metric to be improved is speed it might make sense to move the departments into the same location.

If the metric that is the target for improvement is cost, then maybe relocating from central city-based offices to cheaper 'out-of-town' business parks may be more cost effective.

Level 2 – Operational Departmental Processes. This includes:

- Departmental areas where this stage of the lifecycle takes place
- Deliverables and Dependencies
- Stakeholders
- KPIs and Reporting in terms of Frequency and Distribution

This will cover the identification of the departments involved in the process. Often Level 2 will be used when the 'To Be' planning begins, as it is not uncommon that a department will be identified as being 'responsible' for a new step or process, but at that stage an individual role has not been identified.

This level will include the dependencies and deliverables of each stage of the process. The drawing below has been taken from the retail example used earlier. This is the 'Range plan creation' stage described in 8.2.

All Stakeholders will be included in a level two drawing. This might include external parties if required, and the contracts that underpin the process may also be included. The amount of things 'included' will often depend on the applications used to map the process. The figure above has been created using Microsoft Visio, which is more of a drawing application than a process management application. Hyperlinks to documents held elsewhere can be included to assist someone trying to follow the process. Other applications, of which there are many, can hold actual documents, forms and so on. They can allow version control of the forms and documents used so the user will always be looking at the latest version of the form or document.

For more information on the organisations in this market place, I would recommend the annual Gartner Business Process Management 'Magic Quadrant' report.

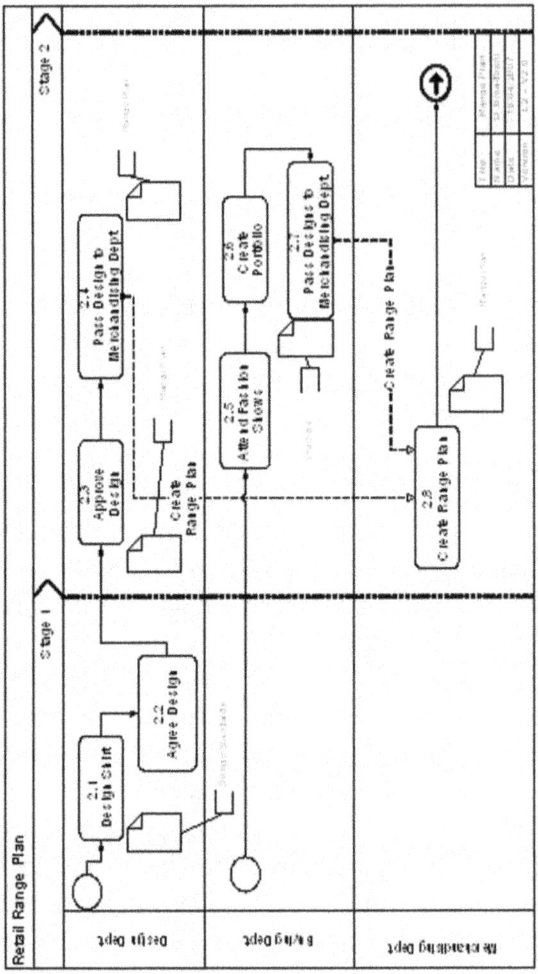

Figure 14 – Level 2 – Departmental Process

As in level 1, level 2 will include reporting. However, at this level reporting is more concerned with frequency and distribution. Therefore, how often these reports are run (daily, weekly, monthly quarterly, etc) and who these reports go to.

As mentioned above, the guideline for all reporting should be that people can make informed decisions based upon the information in the reports. If they are getting information in reports they cannot use to make decisions, then the content of the report or its production should be questioned.

These reports may well be a subset of the reports the senior managers would see at level 1. Only the next level of management may require more detail to make their decisions, so it may be prudent to run these reports more often.

9.1.3 Level Three – Role Processes

At level three we get to the level that describes who does what, where, when and why. The 'where' here corresponds to the location of the person carrying out the role and information on the location, for example there may be security restrictions on a particular location or a maximum number of people who can fit into a location which may have an impact on volume of throughput.

Level 3 – Role Processes. This includes:

- Defined Roles (Grades/Authority, etc)
- Workflow Objects (including scenarios)
- Process Timings (including wait time)
- Business Governance
- Data Element Definitions

Level 3 may often run onto several pieces of paper depending on a number of variables, the amount of detail you need to capture, the complexity of the process, the size of printer or plotter you can use to print the process, and so on. But regardless of the number of pages used at level 3, anyone analysing the process will know that they are looking at a role level of information.

It will include all grades and authorities required to carry out the activities involved in the process. The person carrying out a process needs to be able to do so. For example, in a hospital the process that follows the path a patient goes through on their 'journey' through an operating theatre, will include a number of stages where activities will be carried out by anaesthetist and a surgeon. The defined roles will ensure that the person carrying out these stages of the process is qualified to do so. The process may include sensitive or confidential information and therefore the person carrying out the process may need to have a certain level of clearance before they can carry out the process.

It will include the workflow objects. These are the activities mapped into boxes that describe 'what' the person following the process will do. It will include the decisions that need to be made, depending on the scenario that the user is following through the drawing. It will include the business rules that are being followed to ensure that the user makes the right decisions. Business rules for a process will be signed off by the process owner and regularly reviewed. The rules need to be there to ensure that there is no ambiguity within the process. Users should not have to assume or guess what should be done in a process.

It will include the timings within a process. A process will include both sequential and cumulative timings.

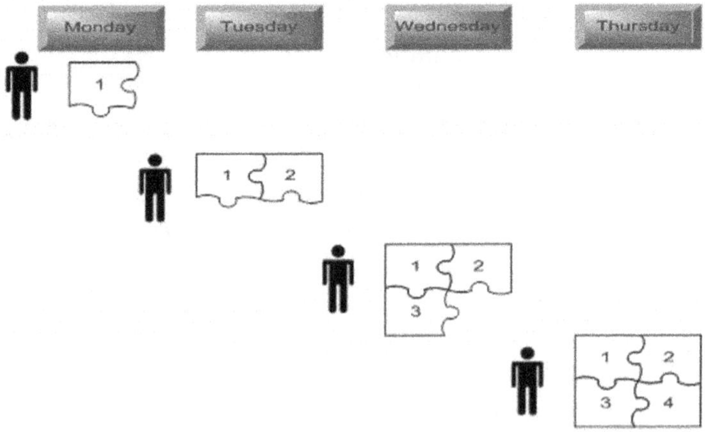

Figure 15 – Sequential and Cumulative timings

The figure above is an example of sequential and cumulative timings. The example follows the creation of a report. The first person does an activity on a Monday that takes one hour. Once this is completed, they send it to the second person via internal post. The second person gets the report on the Tuesday and carries out their activities, which takes another hour, and then puts it in the internal post. The third person gets the report on the Wednesday and carries out their activities, which take an hour and sends it to the fourth person through the internal post. Finally the last person gets the report on the Thursday and adds the final piece of the jigsaw to complete the report, and their activities also take an hour.

Sequentially the process took four hours, however, cumulatively the process took four days. If the metric the organisation was trying to improve was the speed of the process, there might be little that could be done about the four individual stages of the process, so the areas of the process the business analysts would be focusing on would be the internal post to see if the gaps between the handovers could be addressed.

Level 3 will include data element definitions. The definitions of data or 'metadata', as it's sometimes called, will define what data is being collected. For example, data about a person may be described as:

- Name
- Address
    - First line of address
    - Second line of address
    - City
    - County/State
    - Postcode/Zip Code
    - Country
- Date of birth
- Fixed line telephone number
- Mobile telephone number

- Email address
- Nationality

The processes used within an organisation will dictate the level of detail collected, but this is where that level of detail would be detailed. The actual data would be held within other databases.

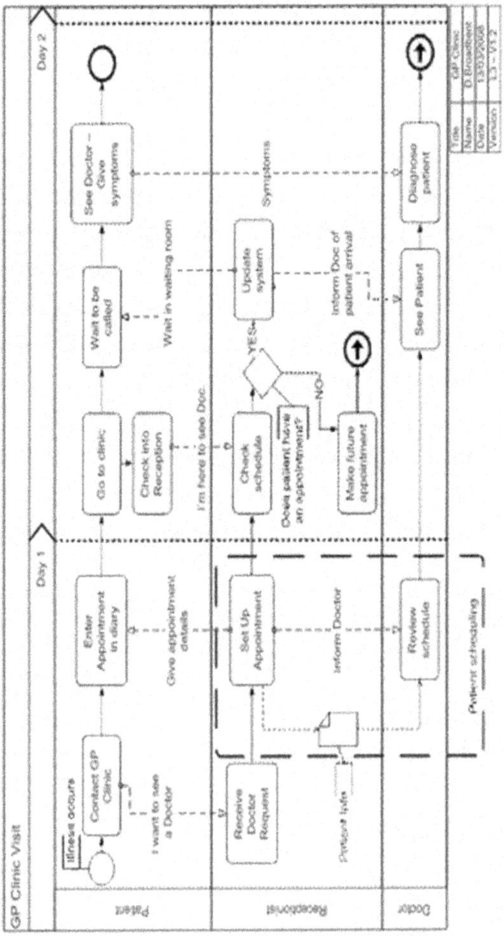

Figure 16 – Level 3 – Role Process

The drawing above is a level 3 process map describing a visit to the Doctor, mapped using Business Process Modelling Notation (BPMN). Each lane has the activities that roles are to perform. It has the communications between the lanes. It has the decision point that needs to be made, the business rule and the information being used in the process and it is under version control.

There is only one decision point in the process above, yet potentially there are four possible scenarios. The first is that the patient has made an appointment and arrives at the correct time; the second is that they have made an appointment but arrive at the wrong time; the third is that they arrive but don't have an appointment; and lastly they make the appointment, arrive on time but the doctor is unable to see them for some other reason.

As mentioned, the amount of information you can hold about a process will vary depending on the application you use to map and store that process. Certain applications will allow the holding of additional information, such as the scenarios involved within a process. Here again I would recommend that the Pareto Principle be followed. The Pareto Principle, or 80/20 rule as it is more commonly known, states that for many events roughly 80% of the effects come from 20% of the causes. Therefore, 80% of the volume that goes through any given process will go through 20% of the scenarios represented on that process. Although there may be many potential scenarios that run through a business process, I suggest you start with the most common or the highest volume scenarios. In this way you will tackle those that will yield the greatest benefit first. You will need to 'exception manage' the other scenarios in the short term, but that would be, in effect, what happens currently in any case.

All drawings created should be done under version control. This will allow copies to be distributed for verification but, when the feedback is received, then updates are added in a controlled manner.

To summarise, we now know who will be doing what, when, where and why, but not how. This is what is held in level four.

9.1.4 Level Four – Functional Dynamics

At level four we capture the 'How' a process is performed.

Level 4 – Functional Dynamic (HOW), this includes:

- Scenarios within the business process
- Applications used
- Systems used
- Screen shots
- Data entry with error codes
- Skills requirements of users
- Security clearance of users
- Authority to approve transactional activities
- Form ownership

Level four would list screen shots for each scenario, the steps that should be followed and the error messages, if incorrect information is used or the application stops for some reason. I'm sure almost all of you will have encountered the standard Microsoft error box shown in figure 15. Many developers of applications will supply this sort of information on USB drives or CDs so the user can have the live application and the tutorial running in parallel until they have got more experience of using the application.

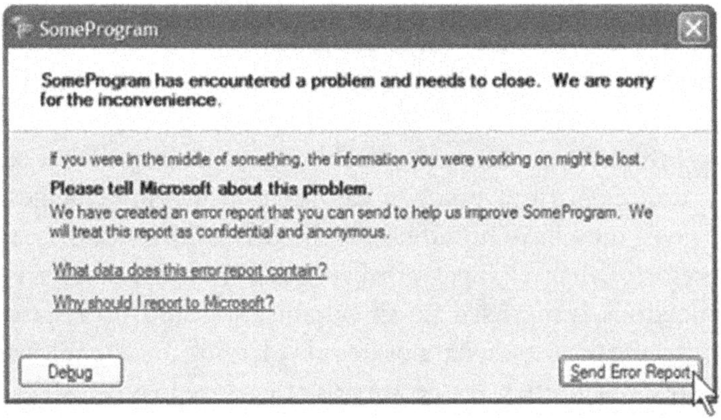

Figure 17 – Error Message

If forms are used in the process, level four would hold a copy of the form as an appendix and have the role or name of the owner of that form and its review cycle.

All of this information on the components that underpin the operational processes needs to be stored. This 'store' is sometimes referred to as an 'Enterprise Architecture'.

9.2 Enterprise Architecture

Enterprise architecture is a description of the structure of an organisation. A formal definition of an enterprise comes from the MIT Centre for Information Systems Research:

'Enterprise Architecture is the organizing logic for business processes and IT infrastructure reflecting the integration and standardization requirements of the firm's operating model.'

Ideally it would be stored in a central location. This idea of a 'single version of the truth' is not new and many application developers have endorsed its advantages. As databases become ever more complex, and the data required to drive complex processes also becomes more complex, there may be practical storage problems with having all the data in a single location.

If you think of an enterprise architecture diagram like a cake with a number of layers, you can see that making changes to one layer may have an effect on the other layers in the cake. Therefore, when changes are being made to the software or applications being used in an organisation and no regard is given to the processes, data or people carrying out the roles and their responsibilities, it's no surprise there are problems.

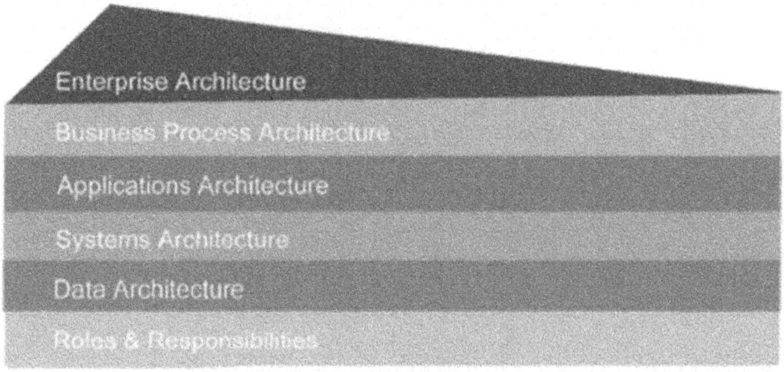

Figure 18 – Enterprise Architecture Model

The elements that comprise an enterprise architecture:

- Business Processes Architecture
- Applications Architecture
- Systems Architecture
- Data Architecture
- Roles and Responsibilities

Business Processes Architecture: This is the business process model, or sometimes referred to as the business operations model. This is the diagrammatical representation of the organisational processes, listing the critical business processes held in the model and the scenarios that each of the maps will cover.

This holds the maps under change control. The documented information underpinning the process maps may include:

- Forms
- Service Level Agreement information
- Operational Level Agreement information
- Underpinning (Back-to-back) Contracts with third parties
- Information about the business goals
- The purpose of the processes
- The volumes the current processes deal with
- The owners of the process
- The business scenarios captured in each drawing
- The governance that covers each process
- Key performance metrics used to measure the process

This information would either be held in the process application the organisation has purchased to support the capture and storage of processes, or stored by other means. This can be achieved by using documents to hold all the locations of the data, and spreadsheets to hold the data about the processes.

Most process mapping applications will export their information into a spreadsheet. See below. The information from the process model fills the first three columns of the spreadsheet. This can then be used to build up a visible picture of the change programme. Any change request is verified against the process model to find out which processes would be affected by the requested change. Change requests which are large enough to be projects in their own right, will have project initiation documents (PID). During the creation of the PID, the person raising the PID will be asked which processes the project will affect. This information can be used to ascertain whether more than one change is planning to affect the same process.

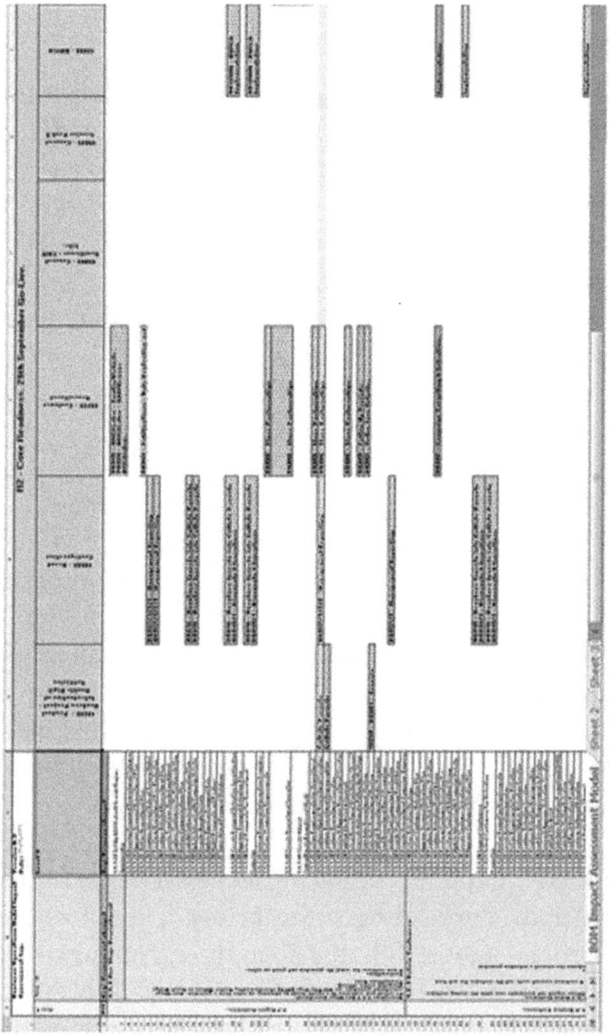

Figure 19 – Export of the Business Process Model

In the diagram above, the highlighted row shows three projects are going to affect the same process. In this case someone from the change team, or the programme office that is responsible for changes, would contact the three people who have raised the change requests to fully understand the impact of the changes on the process. In this way it is easy to establish whether requested changes will work together once they go live, or whether they will be counterproductive to one another.

I would challenge you to see what mechanism currently exists within your own organisation to avoid two projects going live at the same time which will make a working process into a non-working process, because each of the projects was going to try and make the process do something else.

Applications Architecture: These are the applications or software used to carry out the processes, both proprietary and bespoke, who supports them, the maintenance agreements, licence information and so on.

It is probably prudent to mention ITIL at this point. ITIL – The Information Infrastructure Library is a set of concepts and policies for managing information technology (IT) infrastructure, development and operations. Organisations who are attempting to attain the international standard for IT Service Management ISO/IEC 20000 compliance will need to have followed the ITIL framework.

Version 3 of ITIL has within it a number of definitions that would recommend where items such as software licenses should be both physically held – 'A Definitive Media Library' – and where the information about its contents should be held – 'A Configuration Management System' and 'Service Knowledge Management System'.

I refer to ITIL at this point because a number of organisations will have or are planning to implement some form of ITIL-based structure. Where the Enterprise Architecture would differ from what ITIL recommends is that it will hold information about the end-to-end processes, which would encompass other areas of the organisation outside IT, which is where ITIL is focused. Therefore, I would recommend that if your organisation has a Configuration Management System that holds the applications architecture information, then it would make sense to refer to the configuration management system rather than to duplicate the information.

Systems Architecture: This refers to the systems or hardware that the applications are held on and run on. This will include Desktop PC's, Laptop PC's, Servers, Local Area Network equipment (LAN), Wide Area Network equipment (WAN), communications switches, printers, scanners, copiers, fax machines, telephones, palm devices, iPhones, iPads Blackberries, and basically anything that may be used to access and use the business processes.

As above, information on these 'assets' – or 'configuration items' as they are called – may be held in a 'configuration management system' if ITIL is being deployed. By UK law, organisations must hold an 'asset register' which catalogues what they have spent their money on. This is usually held by Finance and may have what has been bought, but may not state where the asset currently is.

Under UK Health and Safety Regulations, UK organisations also have to carry out Portable Application Testing (PAT). This compulsory exercise is easier to perform if the location of every piece of IT an organisation has bought is known. If the testing is carried out by a third party, then the information they provide of what they have tested and where it was situated, can be cross-referenced against the information on the database.

So there are potentially other areas where this information may be held, but it is likely that the interrelationships between them will not be held. This was the ambition of the second version of the ITIL, that the then titled Configuration Management Database would be a single entity which would hold both all the information on the individual 'Configuration Items' and their inter-relationships. In the latest Version Three of ITIL, it has been decided that this is probably not practically achievable and now recommends that, as organisations will have multiple databases, they need only record what databases they have and what they hold.

This may be a step forward in practical terms and may bring the aspirations of ITIL into closer harmony with what is being achieved in the 'real world', however, when an organisation goes through large scale change, the interrelationships between the various parts of the enterprise architecture will need to be established because they will impact on each other.

Data Architecture: Data architecture describes the data structures used by a business and/or its applications. This will include metadata and taxonomy. Metadata is the descriptions of what data is held in any given database, as opposed to the raw data itself. An example of this may be a form that is used in a process. The Metadata will be the field descriptions, so that everyone using the form knows the data that is gathered on it. Taxonomy is the terminology used, so that anyone using the data uses the same meaning of any term. For example, in the National Health Service someone using the service may be called a 'Service User', or a 'Client', but most people would know them better as a 'Patient' so the taxonomy will ensure data terms are not getting mixed up.

There are descriptions of data in storage and data in motion; descriptions of data stores, data groups and data items; and mappings of those data artefacts to data qualities, applications, locations, etc.

Data Architecture describes how data is processed, stored, and utilised in a given system.

Data Architecture breaks a subject down to the atomic level and then builds it back up to the desired form. The Data

Architect breaks the subject down by going through three traditional architectural processes:

- Conceptual – represents all business entities.
- Logical – represents the logic of how entities are related.
- Physical – the realisation of the data mechanisms for a specific type of functionality.

Roles & Responsibilities: This covers the people who actually carry out the processes. It holds the volume of people an organisation has in any particular role, carrying out a process in its 'As Is' status. This may be an important factor as to why there is a bottleneck or constraint within a particular department. Therefore, it will hold or be able to link to organisational hierarchy charts.

It covers the key performance indicators each role has, as this is also a major factor in the way that people behave.

It will hold the security, skill and authority levels for each role. This might include levels of sign-off for projects or changes. Certain roles will only be carried out by people with the relevant security clearance to carry out that role, due to the nature of the data used within the process. Other processes may require a particular skill set for the person carrying out the role; this might include physical skills or training on a particular piece of software. An example of physical skills would be if the process of a patient going through an operating theatre was being mapped, then the activities carried out by the surgeon would be captured. When reviewing or changing the process, these activities would still need to be carried out by someone who was qualified to do so.

When changes are made to processes, the RACI principle can be used. RACI stands for Responsible – Accountable – Consulted – Informed. In the change cycle a number of roles may be involved, the RACI principle gives each role a definition for the amount of input and responsibility it would hold in any given change.

In Appendix A there is the more detailed list of organisational components used in exercise 1. This can be used as a tick list when analysing the amount of information an organisation currently holds about its business or operational processes. It is unlikely that you would find documented evidence of all the component information for an end-to-end process.

9.3 Mapping Standards

One of the major problems in being able to interpret maps drawn by other people is the lack of standards. In the world of Project Management, PRINCE2 is an international standard, therefore it makes sense that if you want to run a project you have all those involved qualified in PRINCE2 so that everyone will understand the terminology and methodology being used.

For many years this was not the case for business process analysis and re-engineering. Plenty of people have been through the 'large roll of brown paper and hundreds of Post-it notes' methodology of capture. There were no industry standards in mapping. To a large extent it simply depended on who you employed to capture your processes, or the package you bought. The major problem with this approach was when that person left the organisation, nobody would be able to interpret the maps. Additionally the maps were not kept up-to-date, so large sums of money were spent on creating maps of processes that were no longer accurate depictions of the actual processes being followed.

This form of expensive wallpaper led a number of organisations to get together in 1989 and the creation of the Object Management Group (OMG).

Founded by eleven companies (including Hewlett-Packard, IBM, Sun Microsystems, Apple Computer, American Airlines and Data General), OMG tried to create a heterogeneous distributed object standard. They created the Business Process Management Initiative and, over the next sixteen years, they eventually agreed a number of standards. The Object Management Group was set up as a not-for-profit organisation in 1989 to run this initiative and is still today the owner of the standards used, not only for business process mapping standards, but also for many others.

Today over 800 companies from both the computer industry and software-using companies from other industries, are members of OMG. In February 2006 the BPMN Version 1.0 language specification was adopted as a standard by OMG.

In February 2008, this was updated to version 1.1 and further work is ongoing, with version 2.0 being released in January 2011.

The Object Management Group works closely with many other organisations such as the Workflow Management Coalition (WfMC) in the production of notational standards which can be used to ultimately create workflow direct from the drawings alone. At the time of writing this, there have been many advances by organisations such as IBM, Oracle and Fujitsu but none has managed to create an end-to-end platform that will go from a drawing to a cross-functional workflow using multiple applications and keeping all the attachments. However, it is my view that this is simply a question of time and the ability to do this will come.

I am not going to go into any greater detail of the work that is currently underway to achieve this. For more information, I would point the reader to the WfMC website where much more information can be found.

Once these organisations had agreed on a standard, 'Business Process Modelling Notation' – or BPMN as it is more commonly known – was born. There are many books written on BPMN, but its two chief architects are Derek Miers and Stephen A White PhD, so if you require reference material I would recommend reading their work, 'BPMN Modelling and Reference Guide'. Or the full guide can be downloaded from www.omg.org for free.

The principal guideline is that drawings should not be so complex that the audience it is aimed at cannot understand it. To accommodate this, BPMN has a number of high-level symbols that can describe simple process maps.

Within these symbols, additional symbols can be added to give those mapping and reading maps additional information.

9.3.1 Business Process Modelling Notation (BPMN)

BPMN uses the following categories and sub-categories:

- Swimlanes
  - Lanes
  - Pools
- Flow Objects
  - Events
  - Activities
  - Gateways
- Connections
  - Sequence flows
  - Message flows
  - Association flows
- Artefacts
  - Data objects
  - Text annotation
  - Groups

9.3.1.1 Swimlanes:

Figure 20 – BPMN Swimlanes

Swimlanes are where the activities a role performs will be. There are two forms of swimlane. The first is a single lane and the second is a pool. The difference between a lane and a pool is that a pool can contain more than one lane.

In the example above in Fig 20, I have mapped a visit to the doctor. The patient has their own lane whereas the Receptionist and the Doctor, although they also have their own lanes, are collectively within the pool that is the General Practitioners' Clinic or GP Clinic.

This would enable someone not familiar with the process to instantly see that the Doctor and Receptionist are in the same place.

9.3.1.2 Events:

Events are the starts and ends of processes. A process must begin with an event and end with one. BPMN allows for intermediate stops along the route, as parallel processes may come into play which have been mapped elsewhere.

The Object Management Group definition of an Event is:

An event is something that 'happens' during the course of a business process. These events affect the flow of the process and usually have a cause (trigger) or an impact (result). There are three types of Events, based on when they affect the flow: Start, Intermediate, and End.

As the name implies, the Start Event indicates where a particular process will start.

An Intermediate Event occurs between a Start Event and an End Event. It will affect the flow of the process, but will not start or (directly) terminate the process.

As the name implies, the End Event indicates where a process will end.

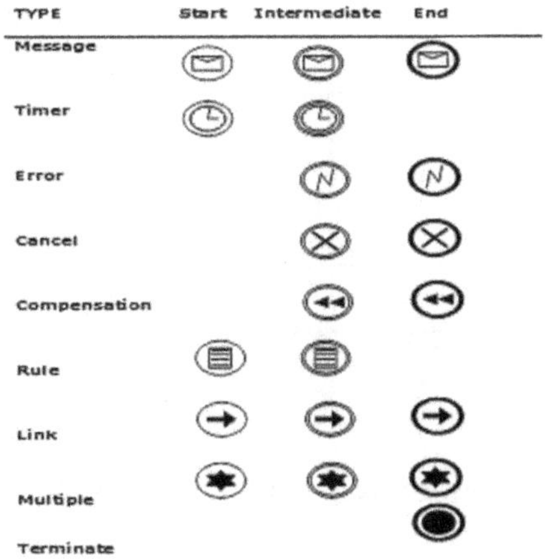

Figure 21 – BPMN – Events

As Fig 21 above shows, there can be a number of additional symbols inside the basic Start, Intermediate and End symbols.

These additional symbols allow the Business Analyst to add additional detail when mapping processes.

These additional symbols can be used when the drawings are presented to a business audience, but I would not always recommend this. The beauty of BPMN is that you can develop a drawing based on the audience it is going to be delivered to. For an audience that would not understand lots of additional symbols, the basic start or finish may be sufficient; Fig 22 below shows a process diagram representing a visit to the doctor and the events shown are one start and three ends. Two of the ends have the additional arrow inside the circle that denotes a 'Linked End', therefore this process finishes but it kicks off another process.

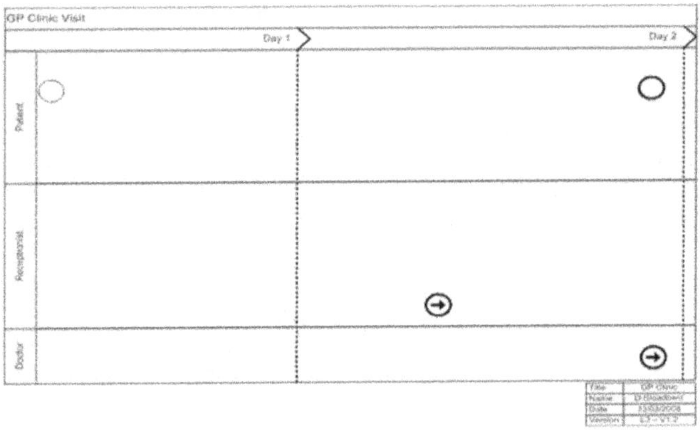

Figure 22 – Events in lanes

The events define the scope of the drawing and will be used in the descriptions of the scenarios used in a process.

We can apply the Pareto Principle, or 80/20 rule as it is more widely known, to the scenarios that will go through a process. Using this rule we can imply that eighty per cent of the volume will go through twenty per cent of the scenarios through any given process, and this is important when both mapping and re-engineering a process. The danger of attempting to map every possible scenario during the initial capture of a process is that the map will firstly become over-complex, and secondly there is the risk that you may never get to the end of the map.

It is therefore my recommendation that before a process is mapped, the scenarios that are to be included are agreed. Scenarios outside of this will be dealt with by exception management. This will assist in tightening the scope of the drawing. I would also recommend that no more than around six scenarios should be looked at initially. This should ensure sufficient detail is captured about the process without making the map over-complex.

9.3.1.3 Activities:

Activities are rounded rectangles. An activity is a generic term for a piece of work or task that someone, or a department, or a company, will perform as part of a process.

In the figure below, the activities have been mapped at role level. BPMN allows sub-processes to be represented in a drawing by adding a '+' symbol to the activity.

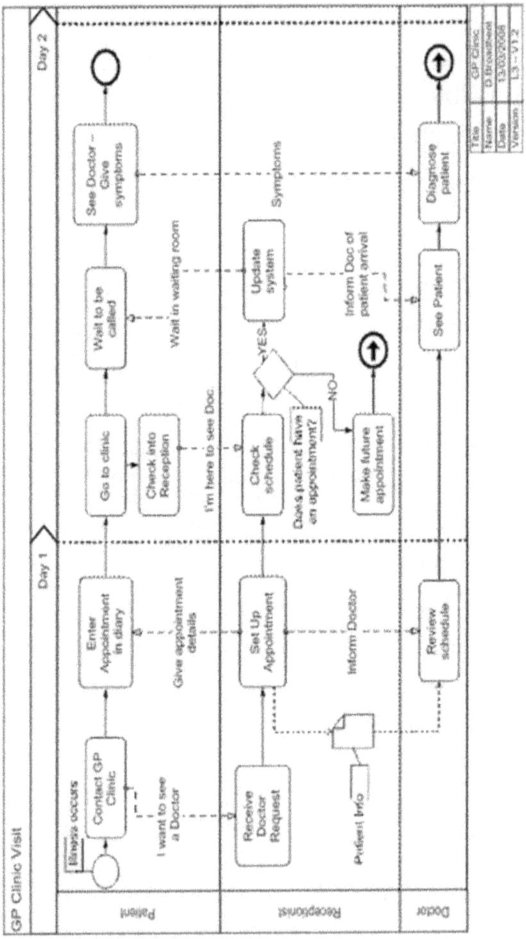

Figure 23 – BPMN Activities

9.3.1.4 Gateways:

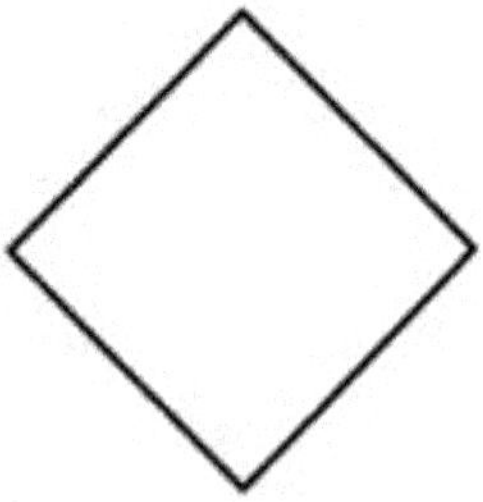

Gateways control the convergence and divergence in processes. Where any decision is required, a gateway will be used. However, it is not only used for decision points.

The Object Management Group definition of a Gateway is:

'A Gateway is used to control the divergence and convergence of multiple sequence flows. Thus, it will determine branching, forking, merging and joining of paths. Internal markers will indicate the type of flow behaviour control.'

Within many methodologies, the diamond shape is used to represent decision points. However, the diamond has a drawback in that it only has four points. Therefore, if you have one input then you have a maximum of three outputs. For this reason O.M.G. decided to keep the diamond symbol but will allow multiple lines to come from one.

In the same way as the Events symbol, there are additional symbols that can be used within the diamond to demonstrate different conditions.

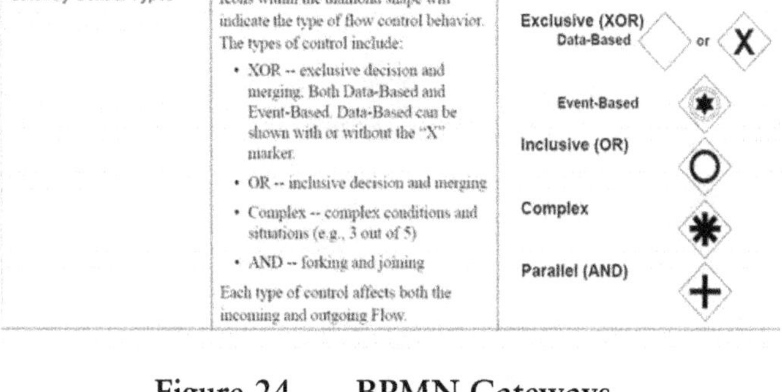

Figure 24 – BPMN Gateways

As mentioned earlier, for every decision there should be a business rule. That is one of the key reasons that processes should have owners, so that there is a position within the organisation that is accountable and responsible for the governance of the process, how often it is reviewed, by whom, what metrics are used, and so on.

9.3.1.5 Connectors:

There are three types of connectors used in BPMN diagrams: those that represent sequence flows, those that represent message flows, and those that represent associations.

Sequence Flow:

A sequence flow is used to show the order in which activities will be performed within a role or lane in a process. This will differ from process scenarios, as a scenario can cross multiple lanes or pools. Sequence flows will stay within a lane.

Message Flow:

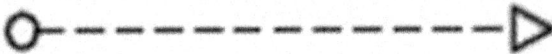

A message flow is used to show the flow of messages between two participants that are prepared to send and receive them within a process. This will be between swimlanes or pools.

Association:

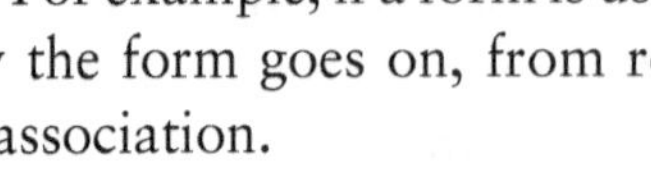

An association is used to show the progress of data objects within a process. For example, if a form is used within a process then the journey the form goes on, from role to role, can be shown using an association.

9.3.1.6 Data Object:

A data object is something that the process uses to hold data. It is not a process of itself; the symbol used is:

For example, a data object can be any of the following:

- Paper document or form
- Dropdown list
- Electronic form
- SMS/Text message
- Email
- Spreadsheet
- Voicemail
- Report
- Database

The symbol is a piece of paper with the corner folded down. It is not unusual for a number of differing data objects to be used within a process so, to avoid confusion, if you have access to a colour printer you can use different colours to represent different data objects.

BPMN is a recognised international standard used by all leading organisations which are developing applications that can be used for business process mapping, re-engineering and management.

The long term goal is to go from a drawing to workflow without any human coding required in between, and plenty of

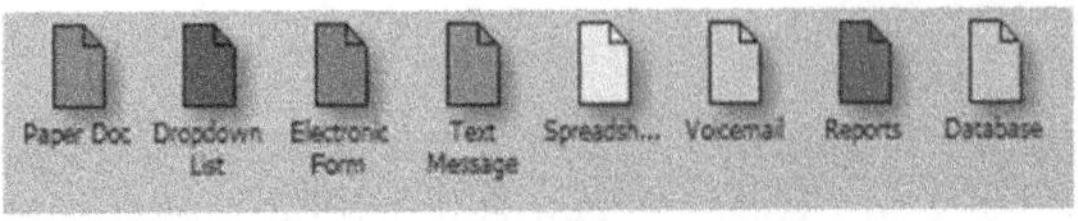

Figure 25 – Types of objects that can hold data

money is being spent in research and development to achieve this.

As mentioned, at the time of writing there has been a great deal of work carried out by a number of leading companies to develop XPDL (Cross-functional process definition language). This is the glue that will sit between BPMN and BPEL (Business process executable language), which is a web-based language that will allow the execution of a process without any additional coding required.

At time of writing, plenty of work has been done but a universal solution has not been agreed, however, it is my belief that it is simply a matter of time before this becomes a reality. The Workflow Management Coalition (WfMC) is one of the leading forces driving these standards.

9.4 Timeline Analysis

BPMN will capture the activities that are undertaken but not the time it takes to do them. This is an additional activity.

In section 9.1.3 Fig 15, sequential and cumulative timings are described. There are plenty of packages on the market that will run as a background task logging each time a PC is logged into and for how long.

If none of these applications are available, a simple spreadsheet can be used to log the sequential timings of activities.

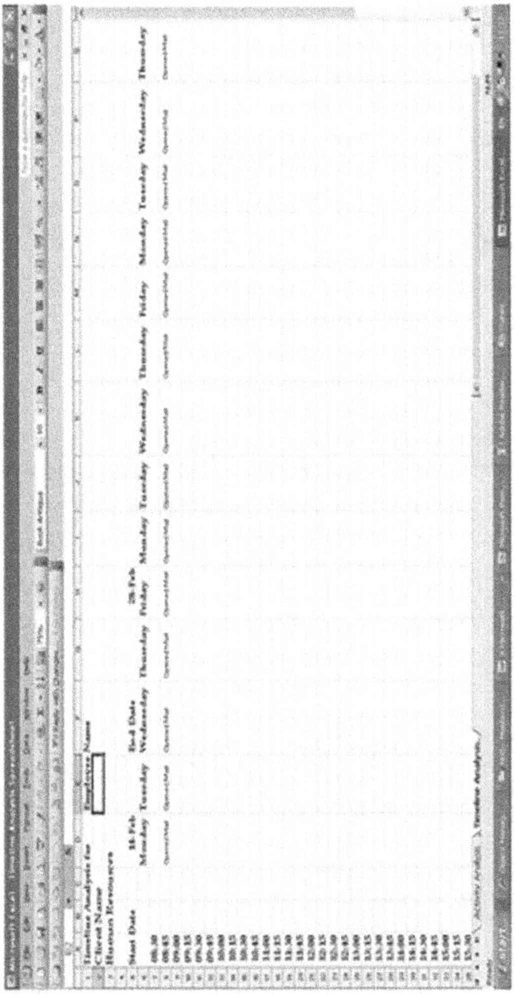

Figure 26 – Timeline Analysis

The figure above is a spreadsheet split into sections of fifteen minutes. It is done in this way because fifteen minutes equates to three per cent of a standard working day. It might be difficult to recall off the top of your head what you were doing three weeks ago last Thursday, unless you are either phenomenally well organised or you were involved in an all-day activity.

This simple method can be activated by having your calendar ping you every fifteen minutes with the action 'what have you been doing?'.

This information can then be fed into other spreadsheets where that data can be used in conjunction with a person's salary, their related overhead costs and the hours that person works in a week. This will give an accurate 'activity-based costing' for each activity carried out by that person (see below).

There are many of these types of spreadsheets about, but some of them start with a predefined list of activities a person is involved in and ask the person to split the 100% of their time across the activities they perform. The problem with this approach is that it is subjective. The person is likely to end up with more than one hundred per cent the first time they fill in the sheet and then shave amounts off each activity until it fits one hundred per cent. Therefore, it is not an accurate measure of what they do.

Actually logging a person's time ensures that the information fed into this spreadsheet is accurate. The longer this method is used the more accurate it will be become, but initial information can be gained by using it for as little as two to four weeks. This will not take seasonal variations into account, but will help in identifying where non-productive activities are being undertaken.

It will also allow you to question why certain individuals are getting involved in activities that are either below their skill level or above it. And lastly, it will identify the sequential timings and assist in the identification of the cumulative timings when the information from more than one spreadsheet is compared.

Altogether this information can provide you with the information of what it costs your organisation to carry out its

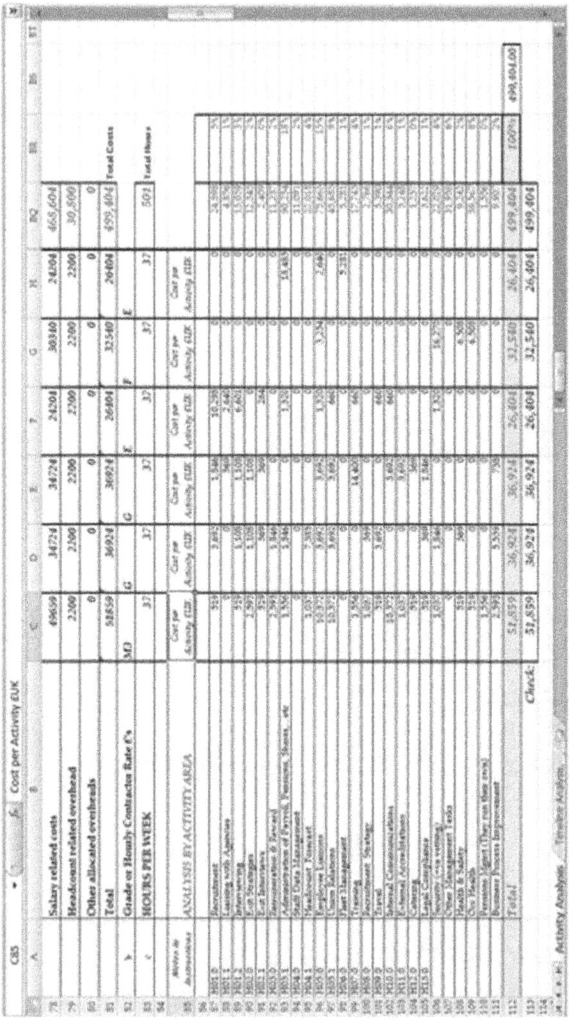

Figure 27 – Cost of Non-conformance Spreadsheet

day-to-day functions. As shown below, this can be shown either as a direct cost or as a percentage of the overall cost. Therefore, it will also provide you with the information of how much it is costing your organisation to do things wrong. This cost of non-conformance is a very powerful argument as to why a process should be changed.

NB. The working version of this spreadsheet will be available at www.samakira.co.uk

9.5 Other Capture methods

There are plenty of other initial capture tools and methodologies that are on the market, but basically there are some standards. All processes will have 'deliverables' – what the process does, what it achieves, and what a stage in a process delivers to the next stage of a process or to other processes. All processes will have 'dependencies' – what the process needs to be able to carry out the process in terms of data, applications, subject matter experts and environment.

To summarise, you will need to be able to capture the following:

A) You want to be able to capture what the inputs or dependencies and outputs or deliverables of a process are, in terms of type and content.
B) You want to be able to capture the volume of inputs or dependencies and outputs or deliverables of a process.
C) You want to be able to capture the roles that are involved in a process.
D) You want to be able to capture the volume of roles involved in a process.
E) You want to be able to capture where the inputs or dependencies come from.
F) You want to be able to capture where the outputs or deliverables go to.

How this information is captured is open to your individual budget, resources available, and so on. Flip charts and rolls of paper covered in Post-its are perfectly acceptable ways of facilitating a workshop to collect the initial data, but something else would be needed to reflect back the findings. Yet this doesn't have to be an expensive process mapping application. Most desktop applications will allow you to draw these pictures, but I would recommend you invest in an application that can capture your operational processes and store them in a Business Operations Model (BOM) using Business Process Modelling Notation (BPMN), as it is the international standard. There are some applications that can be downloaded from the internet to assist in this. For example, at time of going to press www.bizagi.com is an organisation that allows you to download a BPMN compliant modelling tool free of charge.

Quite often just the exercise of getting people into a room to map a process can start discussions about re-engineering the process which would have never taken place if the exercise had not been undertaken. People re-engineer processes, so people will always be a vital factor in the re-engineering of an organisation. This will be demonstrated in the case study in part two.

10 Part Two Introduction

Part one has given the reader the understanding of the Business Process Capability Maturity Model (BPCMM), and the exercises will hopefully have helped the reader establish where his or her organisation is on the learning curve of maturity in establishing and re-engineering their business processes.

It will have given the reader some tools and techniques to map and analyse processes in terms of sequential and cumulative timings. It will have given them tools to collect information about the Enterprise Architecture of an organisation, and an understanding of the components of an Enterprise Architecture that are likely to be affected by change programmes. It has shown the reader the notation standard of BPMN and has demonstrated the stages of the Samakira change cycle approach and the importance of cross-functional communications and senior management buy-in.

It will have shown some of the common pointers to why a number of change projects go wrong, why expectations are often not set, or unrealistic expectations are put upon change teams without the support of senior management from start to finish.

Part two will show the reader how these tools can be put into practice and what part the culture of an organisation plays as a major factor in how it will approach change. The mechanics are a vital foundation, which is why part one is dedicated to getting that foundation in place. However, all too often organisations approach 'change' without taking the organisational culture into account. Change is reactive and cascaded down from senior management or imposed upon a workforce. This will invariably lead to problems and resistance to change.

There may be some passages that are repeated from part one. This is partly a reminder to ensure certain points are remembered, but also in case you have opened the book at this point assuming you didn't need to read the first part.

11 The Journey

To describe the impact that culture has on a change programme, this is a version of the presentations I gave at the Object Management Group's (OMG) European conference on Business Process Management in the Netherlands in November 2008 and at the International Business Process Management Conference in San Antonio, Texas USA in September 2009, turned into more of a narrative.

The presentations were created to demonstrate the effects of culture on a change programme and the impact which culture has on 'resistance to change'. It incorporates real life events that took place in a number of organisations I have worked in. For reasons of commercial confidentiality, this case study does not name the organisations involved but is based on events that took place during change programmes I was personally involved in. I believe the themes discussed are universal.

The study will follow the five stage cycle:

However, first some background:

11.1 Background

In most organisations there are areas that can be identified as not working to their maximum potential. There are areas of an organisation that, should there be a failure of a device, its impact would be instant. For example, if an email server should go down then its impact is felt immediately; people cannot send or receive email. The potential impact of this might be that an organisation might not get orders if they are sent by email, therefore it could have a critical impact on the organisation.

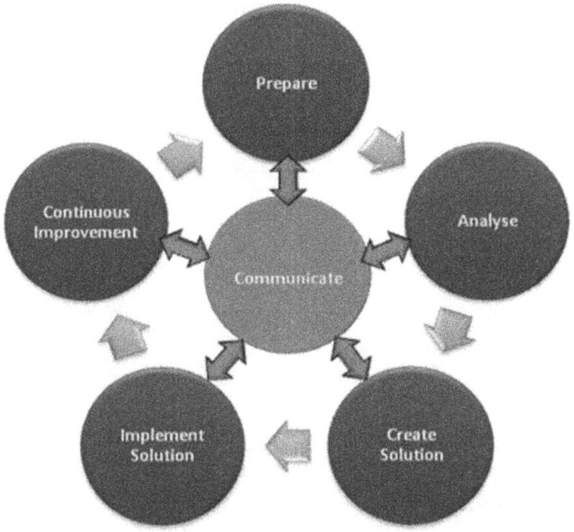

Fig 5 – The Samakira Change Lifecycle Model

When organisations analyse themselves, people are happy to analyse and discuss things such as processes, systems and applications. These are safe areas of the organisation to discuss. But there are things that lurk behind these things which people are a lot less comfortable discussing or analysing the impact of; by this I mean things like a lack of cross-functional communication or co-operation, political in-fighting, silo mentality and blame culture. These things can be just as divisive in undermining the performance of an organisation, but they get left because they are more difficult to analyse and repair. So although people within an organisation know these things exist, they are not tackled and the organisation suffers as a result.

Organisations build resilience into their infrastructure so that if an email server goes down, there are fall-back servers, or the server is part of a server farm and so on, to minimise the impact of a single server going down. It is rare for an organisation to build the same level of contingency and resilience into its processes.

People are the problem and the answer.

11.2 Resistance to change

Before the 'Global Recession', organisations would carry out change but it was often seen as a 'nice to have' rather than a 'must have'. But that has now changed and the landscape will never be the same again. Organisations have been driven to make changes, to do things cheaper, to do things with less people, to do things faster.

As the famous quote from Charles Darwin says;

'*It is not the strongest of the species that survives, nor the most intelligent, but rather the one most responsive to change.*'

Many thought survival of the fittest was about speed, but it's about adaptability and responsiveness, and that includes an organisation's ability to deal with resistance to change.

There may be a number of operational issues that will need to be addressed as a result of the changes you are implementing. You will have chosen the metric you are trying to improve and have started to look at the implications in terms of: Processes, Systems, Applications, Data, and maybe Roles and Responsibilities. But does your organisation suffer from any of the following issues?

- A lack of Cross-Functional Communication
  - Staff don't know each other
- A lack of Cross-Functional Co-operation
  - Staff don't care about the rest of the company
- A lack of Understanding of the End-2-End Process
  - Staff only focused on their own silo
  - KPIs only within silo, not end-2-end

- A lack of 'Ownership' of End-2-End Process
  - Senior Managers only want to be accountable for what they can control
  - Organisation structured in Silos
- Blame Culture – 'Whose Fault' when Customers complain
- Silo Mentality
- Political in-fighting
- Resistance to Change

If you do, then the chances are you will encounter resistance. As soon as you announce that 'change' is coming, the company rumour mill will roll into action. Its greatest export is the Doom Merchant. We've all seen these people; they live in every organisation, they are the ones with the sandwich board round their neck that reads, 'The end is nigh!'

And it's an easy environment for the Doom Merchant to operate in, because people fear change. The first thing that happens when someone finds out that a change is coming is that they will ask themselves, 'How will this affect me?' They will look at this question in terms of their career if a department or the company is getting merged, their livelihood if there is a risk of redundancy, their lifestyle if they are about to find themselves out of work, or just their general wellbeing if they like the way that things are currently done. If indeed they were the architect of the way things are currently done, they may just – on principle – decide they don't want them changed.

These Doom Merchants are the ones that spread fear and uncertainty about the changes. Fear breeds resentment, and resentment breeds resistance.

There are four types of resistance and we will look at each of them in turn:

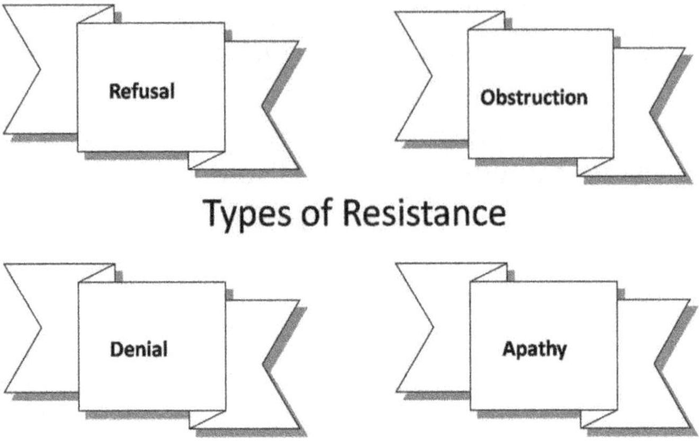

Figure 28 – Resistance to Change

The first one we will look at is Refusal.

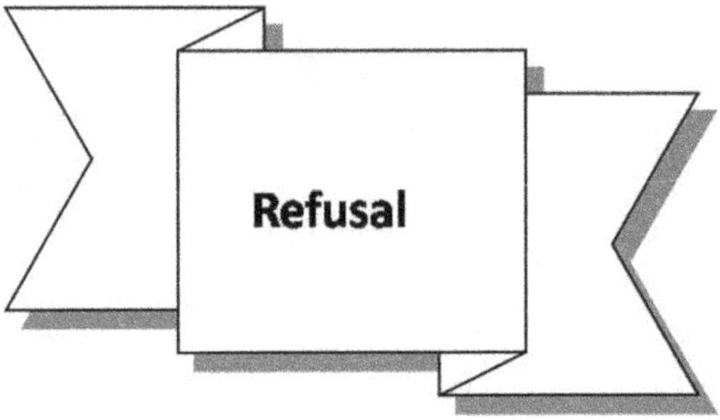

Refusal:

There are two types of refusal resistance, verbal and non-verbal.

With 'Verbal Resistance' there will be some people who believe they are immune to change, that they don't have to get involved if they don't want to, or don't see how this change will further their career or their ambitions. They see no political advantage to get involved, so they decide early on that they won't get involved, they refuse.

This refusal may be vocal, they will tell other people in their peer group that they will not get involved. It increases their self-belief that they are immune because they don't have to change if they don't want to.

Non-Verbal on the other hand is more common. People hear what is being announced and nod in all the right places, but they are only paying lip-service to the change programme. They have decided that they have no interest in the changes, but are not willing to stick their necks out and say so. So they decide they will nod and pretend to go along with the changes but have no intention of implementing the changes. One reason for this is the fear that anything on their resume or curriculum vitae could be seen as a failure. Nobody wants to be associated with anything that fails, so it's safer not to get involved at all. This is ironic when you consider that the vast majority of projects run over-budget or over-time, but on people's cvs they are always to time and budget.

One of the best ways to address verbal resistance is by consistently communicated senior management buy-in. It will be shown in part 2 why this is crucial, but in a nutshell a manager who is displaying verbal refusal is not going to want to help you implement the changes you are trying to. However, if you have senior management (preferably board level) support then the people displaying verbal refusal might not want to assist you, but they do not want to be seen to be getting 'in the way' of a programme.

If they know that the programme you are working on has been communicated as one of the 'top three things the organisation has to achieve this year', then they will need some better arguments as to why they haven't implemented the things they should have.

The section on Approach in part one goes into more detail on the need for gaining senior management buy-in at the start of the programme, but this demonstrates why it is crucial and that, without it, the programme will struggle at best. The buy-in has to be not only from start to finish, but also communicated in such a way that everyone in the organisation knows the profile of the programme and where it sits alongside any other initiative that is being followed.

This support also allows you to potentially sidestep the political obstacles. You can simply escalate the issue if this person is seen as a blocker, or is constantly 'too busy' to see you.

If senior management have given the change programme a high priority, then another example of 'buy-in' is that in early communications the senior management sponsor will state that they will get regular reports of those who do not attend meetings. It is then reasonable to ask anyone who is 'too busy' to attend meetings, what they are doing that is more important than the change programme, so this can be escalated to the senior management.

It is likely that senior management will have different priorities as time goes on, hence the insistence at the 'preparation' stage that they communicate their commitment and buy-in and the programme manager or director reminds them of this when there are conflicts of interest and resource is being pulled to other projects.

This is another demonstration of where the organisation sits on the Business Process Capability Maturity Model, the higher up the model the organisation is, the greater understanding the senior management team will have of the commitment and buy-in required to make the change programme a success.

Next is Obstruction.

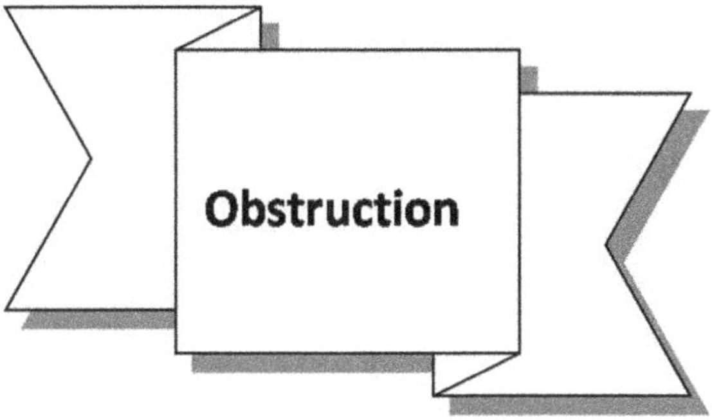

Obstruction:

There are also two types of obstruction, deliberate and non-deliberate.

Deliberate obstruction occurs when, at the start of a business process re-engineering programme, a manager does not fully understand the implications of the programme and has given it their support for political reasons while not really looking at the detail of the plan. They then come to realise that the implementation of the plan will see something that they do not like. For example, the programme might decide that the most cost-effective way to run part of the organisation is to outsource the work to a third party, and as a result this will lead to a significant reduction in head count of his or her department. This will be interpreted as a reduction in that person's political power and influence and then they will not be as supportive as they might initially have been.

Things will start to be put in the way of the programme. Resource won't be available because they are 'too busy' running the day-to-day business. Funding might suddenly no longer be available or will 'have to be used for something else'. The manager will raise questions about whether the organisation can really afford to spend all this money on change. What appear to be sensible business questions will be raised to create doubt and delay.

Therefore, it is important to try and assess the potential political impact of the changes that are forecast and discuss these with the senior management sponsor, so potential obstruction can be detected early and dealt with early.

Non-deliberate obstruction is the most common form of resistance to change and it's nothing personal. One of the findings of the 2008 white paper published by the Economist Intelligence Unit and Logica Management Consulting, titled 'Securing the value of business process change', was that one of the main barriers for effective business process improvement was the 'Pressure of day-to-day business'.

This is not a pre-meditated resistance to change in the same way as the others, but it stops change happening nonetheless. Where it drifts into culture is that those who fear the change deep down, or have been worried by the Doom Merchants, do nothing to stop day-to-day business getting in the way of the change programme.

Also, the pressure of day-to-day business is a useful excuse for a 'deliberate obstruction' manager to use to deny resource to a change programme, but it also genuinely happens in a non-deliberate environment. It is very difficult to get people out of their day jobs long enough to re-engineer their day jobs, particularly if they are expected to do those day jobs as well.

One of the causes of 'Non-deliberate obstruction' is when a programme or project does not have sufficient preparation and therefore does not get the visible level of 'senior management buy-in', or does not have a high enough level communication plan. The consequence of this is that the programme is seen just as a 'flavour of the month' and, as such, will be overtaken by other projects. It will simply slip down the pecking order for resource and funding.

A common issue is that many change programmes are reactive in nature. Therefore, insufficient planning has taken place, therefore insufficient senior management buy-in has been sought. The organisation has not fully understood the resource requirements of the programme or project and, as these things become apparent, the required resource is not available. Additional funding is not available for additional resource, so the programme or project takes longer. The focus moves to other projects and programmes. This exacerbates the problem as more demands are put on the same resources continuing the cycle.

In the same way as 'refusal', the communicated commitment of the senior management team and the evidence of buy-in from start to finish is the best remedy for this form of resistance to change. Hopefully you will now be starting to see how crucial the buy-in from senior management is. It's my experience that many senior managers do not fully appreciate the amount of work it will take to deliver a change programme. As demonstrated by the Economist/Logica white paper mentioned above, too many managers assume people can take on the huge task of re-engineering the business from end-to-end, while still doing their day jobs, and often with little or no external expert assistance. It's little wonder that people struggle.

The most effective way to deal with non-deliberate obstruction is to have dedicated a team of people to the programme. At their BPM Conference in London in 2009, Gartner stated that the organisations that were the most effective in implementing both initial change and continual improvement were those organisations that had dedicated change teams, which leads us inevitably back to preparation.

Many surveys over the years keep throwing up the fact that in post-project reviews, one of the issues highlighted again and again is that more preparation should have been done, but it's a lesson rarely heeded.

However, if this has already occurred in your programme, the only course of action is to stop. Call a meeting with the senior management sponsor and explain the situation that more planning needs to take place and the likelihood that some aspect of the scope is probably going to be affected. The outcome might be that the project or programme has to stop until another project that is using the same resource has been completed. Bad as this may seem, at least everyone will be aware of the situation. Expectations can be re-set, rather than believing things will 'sort themselves out'.

It might only need the addition of certain resources for a short period of time, which might be achievable by using things like overtime payments to get a programme back on course. However, I would sound a note of caution here. I do not believe all problems can be solved by simply throwing resource at them, not all solutions are scaleable. As the old adage goes, 'if I get a woman pregnant we have a baby in nine months, if I get nine women pregnant I don't get a baby in a month.' Sometimes things have to be done in order and more resource is not going to speed things up. For example, it might be that a certain piece of software or hardware has to be used and for some reason there is a delay in it turning up. In that case, escalation can be used, but resource would not automatically help.

To sum up, both deliberate and non-deliberate obstruction can be addressed by better communication and planning, but fundamentally the programme has to be supported by visible buy-in from senior management.

Next is Denial

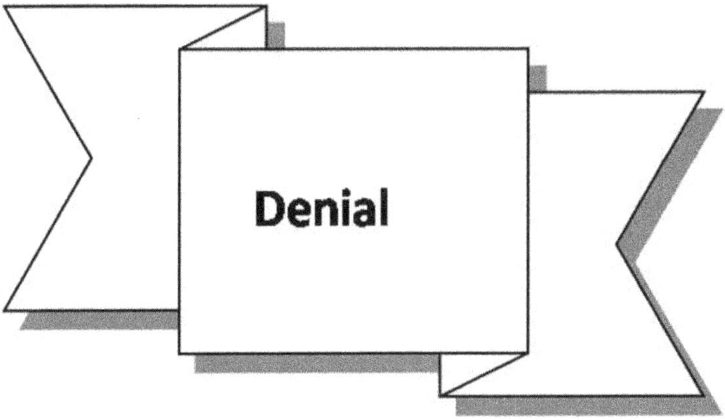

Denial:

On a number of occasions I have stood up in front of senior managers or boards of directors and presented the change plan milestones. People round the table have asked questions until everyone is satisfied and, when asked if everyone is comfortable for the programme to commence, all agree.

As the meeting starts to break up I will approach a senior manager or director and ask them when they have some free time in their diary to discuss how this will affect their department. The vague look of shock flicks across their face and a friendly arm is put around my shoulders as they say, ‘“David, my friend, my department’s fine’, and with a swath of their hand they continue, ‘It’s all these others you have to change.’. The fact that they sat through the presentation which had their department on it can sometimes make no difference. This is simply a level of denial that there could possibly be anything ‘wrong’ with their department. This is sometimes because people would see this as a personal failure if someone external had to come in and ‘fix’ their department.

One issue might be that the current internal key performance indicators may not show that there is anything poor about that department's performance, in fact changes may have been made to improve that individual department against an internal key performance indicator. However, business process analysis may have found that the impact that department has on one further down the end-to-end process is profound, and by default they may have made the end-to-end process less efficient than it was before. But if this has never been measured then nobody will know. Additionally this department will need to make changes to improve the end-to-end process.

Preparation, communication and buy-in are again major factors in addressing this form of resistance. It needs to be made very clear by senior management that not to change is not an option. I do not pretend that this is an easy message to sell, and it will be an early demonstration of the senior management's commitment to the programme when they publish such a communication to the organisation and stand by it the first time a case of 'denial' raises its head.

The solution also has to be 'sold' back to the senior manager. The demonstration that an end-to-end process does not work, but not because of any individual's 'fault', but more from a lack of understanding of the end-to-end process by those involved in it, will do more to bring round a manager because they will no longer feel singled out. They are not being criticised as an individual, they simply own a chunk of an end-to-end process that is not running as efficiently as it should. They need to be able to see how the changes will make the end-to-end process more efficient and then they can go and brag about how well they have done making their department even better.

Prior to the recession, when I used to run business process workshops, in the part where I would discuss resistance I would only mention these three common types. However, since the recession a fourth probably now needs to be mentioned and that is Apathy.

Apathy

Apathy:

Albert Einstein is quoted as having once said, 'The world is not dangerous because of those who do harm but because of those who look at it without doing anything.'

Apathy is something that creeps across an organisation like a dark cloud and, if left unchecked, can consume a great deal of it.

In times of recession where redundancies are commonplace, there might be a period where people slip into what is known as 'survival mode' and these instincts will make people work harder in the short term to avoid being selected for redundancy, even if this has nothing to do with the redundancy selection process.

After those selected for redundancy have left, there is initially a period of relief among those who survived. But when the additional workload of those who have gone is placed upon those remaining, the pressure begins to increase. Morale can start to drop and, if left unchecked, it can turn into apathy.

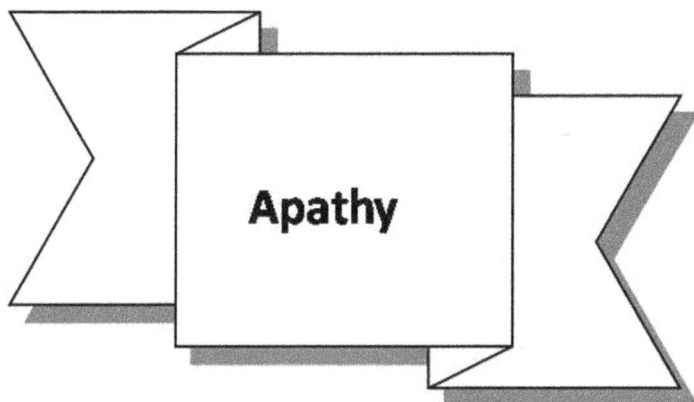

Almost any organisation that has had to go through a round of redundancies has seen its effects, particularly if, as a result of the recession, that organisation has had to go through more than one round of redundancies. Organisations may have to cut costs, which is often the fundamental driver behind cutting headcount, but that company will still have contractual obligations to deliver to its customers. This means the same amount of work will have to undertaken by less people, which can increase the apathy.

People can become 'punch drunk' by rounds of redundancies and the additional stress that the expectation of the same, or a higher, level of performance from less staff can bring. This increases individuals' stress levels to the point where they really don't want to work there any more. But there aren't any other jobs to go to, so they can't just leave. This leads to lower and lower spirits, until the individual gets to the point where they just do not care about the job they are doing, or who they are working for. It is simply a means to pay their rent or mortgage, to keep food on the table and the wolves from the door.

At this point people are particularly vulnerable to the Doom Merchants, who will be spreading fear that there could be more redundancies. Phrases like, 'We've seen it all before' or, 'it will come to nothing' are used to describe the change initiatives and are used to create more uncertainty.

Into this environment comes the announcement that there will be changes and that the senior management are looking for people to be involved in the change programme. It's not a surprise that very few, if any, will put their hand up and say they have 'free time' on their hands to get involved in anything other than their day job. They keep their heads down and just do as they're told.

I believe that apathy is probably the single most difficult type of resistance to change to tackle, particularly in these times. It's very difficult for a senior manager to stand up with any conviction and say that the 'times ahead are rosy'. Nobody really knows how long this recession will take, so forecasting growth is very difficult.

Tackling apathy starts with dynamic leadership. Those in senior positions need to spend the time planning a change programme so it is given the best chance of success. They need to then ensure the resource will be made available to deliver the change programme.

One of the first ways to approach apathy is to make the people affected by the change part of the team bringing about the changes. If people affected are part of the solution, then they are less likely to feel as though the changes are being imposed upon them. If a person can not only see that there is a light at the end of the tunnel, but also knows that their own personal efforts can bring that light closer, then they are going to feel they have more of a personal investment in bringing about that change.

Enthusiasm is the greatest tool to beat apathy, but enthusiasm needs momentum. There is a school of thought that I agree with that states that the first change 'deliverable' has to have been delivered to the organisation within seven to twelve weeks of the programme kicking off or the programme will not be seen as a success and any initial enthusiasm will be lost. So it's important that the team involved are not too ambitious to start with.

So on the one hand, you require momentum and enthusiasm, yet on the other hand you need to temper this so it's not so ambitious, bites off more than it can chew and can't deliver something in the seven to twelve week timescale.

As I have mentioned, I believe the best approach is for the change team to deliver a number of 'change products' to the organisation. It is imperative that the first few of these products do not fail to improve the process and therefore the day-to-day lives of the people running the business processes. This is how to overcome apathy, by motivation and demonstration of commitment.

It will take time; the first few success stories will probably be received with a level of cynicism, and this is to be expected. But if the next change product and the next change product are all delivered to time, and achieve what they were set out to achieve, then some will start to believe in the programme. It might be that some have reached a point where they hope that things will get better but have had nothing to pin those hopes upon. Once a few success stories have been circulated then some will start to hope. Further success will increase the hope and drive out the apathy.

It is therefore vital that realistic expectations are set and then delivered. To an extent this will come back to the senior management buy-in, in releasing resource, in signing off funding, and in communicating the profile of the change programme above anything else that is 'flavour of the month'.

In my experience the way to tackle this is to run a workshop where the change team describes where their department's greatest 'point of pain' is. This may be something to do with a process, an application, a system, the heating/air con, anything, but something emotive to the people of that department. Then find one that can be tackled in the 7-12 week timescale, one that can be achieved with the least effort or cost, and work as a team on that one. Then go from there.

Celebrate and communicate success, this increases the momentum and the more change products the team delivers which actually benefit people on the ground, the more ammunition the team has against the Doom Merchants that the programme is not a waste of time. It won't silence the Doom Merchants, I don't believe this is ever fully achievable, but if the change products can be delivered on time and add value/benefit to the business, then less people will believe the Doom Merchants.

Now follows the case study that will demonstrate these ideas and principles.

11.3 Setting the scene

Resistance to change will appear in different places and to different degrees, and this may be down to how much of a shock it might be that an organisation has to change. For the purposes of this case study, this was an organisation that didn't know it had to change.

It was a telecommunications company. It had offices all over the world and sold fibre to telecommunications companies and other companies round the world. If an organisation wanted its offices round the globe connected, they could buy 'circuits' to connect them.

Internally there were a number of departments involved in the creation of a new circuit, from Sales at the front end all the way through to Finance at the back end raising invoices for ongoing usage or maintenance.

Each of the departments had their own metrics. Key Performance Indicators were used and incentives schemes were based on people's performance against these KPIs. However, each department had been allowed to set their own metrics, therefore, the end-to-end process was not accurately measured.

There were some high level metrics; number of orders per month v number of circuits delivered was one of the 'dashboard' metrics the senior management used. Initially things looked like they were going well, however, customer complaints were rising.

Without making generalisations, some organisations will accept an increase in customer complaints as long as it doesn't affect revenue. But once customer complaints turn into customer cancellations then the alarm bells start to ring.

Circuit provision in the international telecommunications market fell roughly into three categories On-Net, Off-Net and No-Net:

- On-Net – If you were an existing customer and wanted an additional circuit on the company's existing network, it would take roughly thirty days to provision.
- Off-Net – If you were an existing customer of another telecommunications company and it meant buying the circuit from that company and adding to existing circuits from our company, then it would take roughly sixty days to provision.
- No-Net – If your company did not have any circuits and the company would have to dig through fields or streets to get to your office, planning permission would be required, then it would take roughly ninety days to provision.

This thirty, sixty, ninety days for circuit provision were industry standard metrics in a similar way that customer call centres will use PCA10, which equals 'percentage of calls answered in 10 seconds' as an industry standard metric which allows observers of the sector to benchmark companies.

But as it was the customers complaining, I suggested we look at the performance of the company from the customers' perspective. The work began by analysing the circuits provisioned in the November. By looking at the thirty day orders from October, the sixty day orders from September and the ninety day orders from August, we could calculate what expectations had been set to the customers, and then by looking at each of those orders we could see how well those expectations had been met.

The results were that only twelve per cent of orders had met the expectations that had been set. It was no surprise customers were complaining. So we had found out why customers were complaining and cancelling orders, but this raised the question why the internal metrics had not found this out and alerted the company earlier.

The reason was simple; all the metrics were done within the silos, there were no end-to-end metrics. Directors of individual departments felt they should not be accountable for something that was not directly in their control. Therefore, staff were not incentivised to care about the rest of the business. By default, they were actively discouraged from doing so. Not by some disruptive scheme, but by the fact that they concentrated on making their own department more efficient without looking at the possible knock-on effects those changes had on other departments involved in the same end-to-end process.

As described in section one with the new starter process, here there was no end-to-end process ownership. When these figures were presented to the senior management team, it was obvious that changes in the way the organisation was measured would be needed, but getting these changes was not without its challenges. The current metrics model had cost a great deal of money to put in place and there were some who used the phrase, 'they must be right because they cost "x" pounds of consultants' time to create'. This 'Emperor's new clothes' view of services still surprises me, even after all these years. If something is beneficial to an organisation, it is beneficial whether it cost a lot of money or not, therefore, it is equally true that something can be detrimental regardless of how much it cost. It is not a universal truth that just because it was expensive it is right.

Fortunately the project's senior management sponsor saw the value in the work that had been carried out and the findings that were presented. He realised that further work was needed now that we had found out why the customers were not happy and why this information had not been apparent before. He therefore instructed my team thus, 'Ok, now you've found the problem, what's it going to take to fix it?'

Over the next few weeks the scope was refined. The 'what's out' list was almost as long as the 'what's in' list. This was not wasted time, for there were a number of occasions during the life of the project when senior managers tried to get the scope to 'creep'.

At this point I would reinforce that in many cases it is difficult for 100% of the scope to be defined and agreed. If only 80% of the scope can be defined, I would recommend that you make the 80% the 100% and manage any additions under formal change control, where things like additional resource and funding are considered or timelines extended, to ensure that expectations remain realistic.

Finally the scope, resource and funding was formally approved and the programme could begin. For the purposes of this case study, I will take you through each of the sections as chapters.

11.4 Preparation

There will be occasions when stages of the approach may be repeated. In this case, for example, there had been preparation followed by analysis, this led to the conclusion that further analysis was required, therefore, further preparation was required.

In the initial analysis people were interviewed and databases investigated to collect the information to prove that the customers' expectations were not being met. Now that we were going to look to carry out root cause analysis to further investigate the causes and then create a solution, we needed subject matter experts from each of the areas involved in the end-to-end process and support areas of the business.

An important step in the creation of the team was that the senior management were asked to nominate the 'subject matter expert' from the area they were responsible for, and to empower that person with the authority to make decisions for that department. This was not an easy step to complete but was an early test of the senior managers' commitment and 'buy-in' to the programme. Sometimes just the list of names involved in a project will send a message that the senior management are 'serious'.

With all due respect to all individuals that work within departments, and although we should always view people as equals, there will always be those who – through their natural abilities, experience and skills – are more important to the managers of that department than others. Far too often managers are naturally reluctant to give up their 'star players' to a programme that they know will take up a lot of their time and, although statistics are probably impossible to gauge, I'm certain programmes have either performed poorly or failed completely because they were staffed with resource that managers could 'afford' to lose for some time without it impacting the department's ability to continue doing its 'day job'.

Some of the support experts didn't even know themselves why they were involved and did question at the kick-off event why they were present. The most common areas for this are Finance and HR. I told them it would become clear later, but it is worthy of note that Finance, HR and IT are, by their very nature, cross-functional departments, and as most processes where there are problems of ownership are cross-functional, it makes sense to have cross-functional representatives in the team. You will see later how key the HR representative was to this particular programme.

The first meeting of a team often provides a number of good clues. Bruce Tuckman describes groups as going through four distinct stages; these are Forming, Storming, Norming and Performing. Although at the first meeting the group will still be 'Forming', there is subtle storming going on. A lot of this can be seen in the body language of those involved.

I could have spent many pages discussing body language but decided against it, as there are plenty of books on the subject. To quote Allan & Barbara Pease, body language should be studied in 'clusters'. Someone with their arms folded might be cold not defensive, someone rubbing their nose when they speak might have hay fever not be lying, so it's important to not jump to conclusions.

However, it is interesting just to watch the way a room fills up, the way people enter a room, Do they strut in loudly – over confident perhaps? Do they creep in timidly – unsure of why they have been chosen, or uncomfortable in the company of others in the room? People will naturally sit with those they know and feel comfortable with. Look at the distance people leave between them as they get their tea or coffee. A lot can be gleaned about the inter-relationships between these people just by observing how close they allow others to stand within their 'personal space bubble'.

Males will often strut more than females in an attempt to display superiority. I am a firm believer that many males believe in hierarchy even if subconsciously and, if you leave a bunch of men who have never met together in a room, within a very short time they will have discussed what they do, earn, drive, where they live and various other measurements of success to establish who is 'top dog' and where they fit in. Women, on the other hand, are usually far more intuitive and supportive so I find if it is possible I'd recommend you have as close to a fifty–fifty per cent mix of males and females as possible, but of course it might not work out that simply.

Once everyone had settled down, I introduced myself then went round the table and asked people to introduce themselves and state what their role in this process was. Again it was an opportunity to watch them; how they studied the others, some leaned forward nodding along to most of what was being said in supportive body language motions, others would be sitting with folded arms, crossed ankles, pursed lips, sitting as far back in their chairs as it was possible to get, or simply not engaging at all. I make it a rule to have all mobiles, iPhones and Blackberrys off. Other tools can be used defensively, women can put handbags across their bodies or on their laps, or hold a drink in such a way that their arm is across their body.

Sometimes postures like the non-eye contact, looking down and picking invisible lint off clothing, can demonstrate a level of discomfort.

The opposite can also be displayed, the catapult – mostly done by men – with the arms behind the head and the elbows pointing out in a display of arrogant 'I'm in control' has, by some studies in apes, been shown that it is used to make the head look bigger and therefore more intimidating. All these were signals to how far this group had to go.

The fact that they had to introduce themselves is the first clue to the fact that this was the first time all the parties involved in this end-to-end process had been in the same room. Some of these people had worked in the company for over ten years, some in the same building, on the same floor, working on the same process, yet they had never met.

The two clues this gave straight away was there was little or no cross-functional communication. This meant they were used to operating within silos, so I suspected a level of Silo mentality where data and responsibility were 'thrown over the fence' and probably blame culture.

To kick the event off I facilitated the mapping of the high level end-to-end process. I gave everyone in advance of the meeting no more than three minutes to explain:

- What they did.
- What the output of what they did was.
- What their dependencies were.
- Where they saw problems in the process.

This was to give each person the opportunity to talk with authority and because I suspected it might flush out some of the areas where we believed there were problems.

First up was the Salesman, confident as you would expect a Salesman to be. He talked about the sales cycle and how he sent a form into the company that went to Circuit Design. At this point the representative from Circuit Design said, 'I never see that form.'

Very quickly a discussion, or carefully veiled argument, commenced. Another clue that demonstrates a lack of cross-functional communication and co-operation is when people describe another part of the same company as 'they'.

Then the representative from Finance put her hand up, 'We get that form.'

People stopped arguing. 'What do you do with it?' I asked.

'We take the customer's name and address, then throw it in the bin.'

'Why?' I asked, as did others round the table.

'Because nobody has ever asked for it, so we assumed nobody else needed it.'

The arguing started up again. I suspected I wouldn't get to the end of the process, but that didn't really matter at this stage. It is important to try and gauge the level of baggage that individuals have brought into the room.

People will sometimes bring up events from years before, when department X let department Y down and they were personally affected. It is important to let this 'blood on the table' session take place. It doesn't always occur and it comes down to personal judgement when to step in to stop some of the baggage becoming abusive. But it is important, because this team has to ultimately develop the solution and they will never be able to do this if they are at each other's throats and do not trust each other.

Additionally there may be some 'resistance to change'. Particularly the 'non-verbal' refusal type, where someone has been selected for this team, but deep down either doesn't want to be involved in the team, or deep down doesn't want to change the process because it suits them personally quite well as it currently runs. These people will take slightly longer to flush out. You may also come across some representatives who have the 'denial' type of resistance to change, where they can't see where there could be any possible fault with their department, particularly if they have had personal input into the changes that took place within their silo, often regardless of whether it had been proven to enhance the end-to-end process or not. These are areas where I would recommend you get external expertise to assist your organisation, as this organisation was clearly at the bottom end of the business process capability maturity model.

So after I felt everyone had had their chance to vent their spleens about whose 'fault' it was that the process didn't work properly, I told them we were going to map the process formally. Business Process Modelling Notation (BPMN) would be used and the remainder of the event was used to get all of the team up to the same level of understanding of how to map a process.

11.5 Analysis

Following the Zachman framework idea of who does what, when, where, how and why, we agreed to map the process end-to-end at role level.

Once the team had mapped the process, it was printed and put up on the walls of the offices with a request for all staff to have a look at the process and, if there were any anomalies, to put them on a Post-it. After a few days there were so many Post-its that another workshop was called.

This was to be expected; just because two people do the same process doesn't always mean they will do it in the same way. They are not likely to check the way others do their own jobs, people just get on with the work. In my experience, this verification stage will go through between three and six iterations before you reach a process map that has no Post-its on it.

It took five versions before the drawings were free of additions. This was a useful exercise in the forming of the team, because it doesn't do them any harm to be shown that they didn't know their own organisation as well as they thought they did. The process, with all its faults, was then presented to the senior management and they were asked to sign it off as an accurate 'As Is' drawing.

This can take time because often management will be happy to agree that the map reflects their department's processes up to the point you ask them to sign it off. Then they want to go through it with a fine toothcomb. I would always advise the process have a formal 'sign off' because change programmes can take time and if management personnel change it is important the programme does not have to retrace steps.

It is also a common trait for managers to disagree with some of the 'As Is' findings and the phrase to look out for is something like, 'That's not what they should be doing. What they should be doing is...' and they then go on to describe how they think the current process should work. If you do come across this, you need to have the faith in the Subject Matter Experts. If they say that this is the process at the moment, they are the best equipped people to understand the process so that will be the way the process currently runs, whether the management happen to like what they see or not.

Another option is to use process mining tools to gather evidence of the current process. This is only possible if the data on the process can be exported into a process mining tool, but if it can, then a great deal of evidence can be gathered. One of the tools I've seen on the market that does this is from an organisation called Pallas Athena (see www.pallas-athena.com)

We analysed the maximum throughput of each department and one department was clearly a bottleneck:

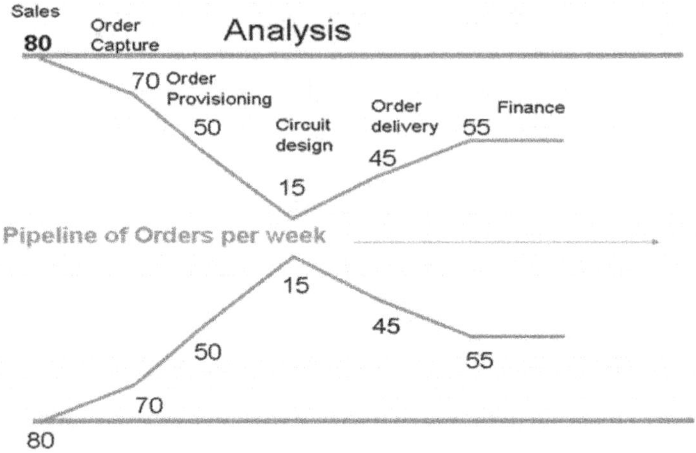

Figure 29 – Throughput Analysis

The analysis found four main things that impacted the process and caused Circuit Design to have a throughput of only 15 per week:

- Four circuit design engineers were sharing two PCs.
- Most of the information they were getting was irrelevant to circuit design and the information they needed they did not get and had to go direct to the customer to get.
- Sales got their bonuses when orders were placed rather than when orders were delivered, so sometimes insufficient information was gathered.
- Forms with free text fields were faxed in, so had to be retyped into the order application.

The reasons for these were as follows: in an effort to save money, the IT and Finance Directors had issued a blanket order that no more IT would be purchased until the beginning of the next tax year. This had caused four people to share two PCs.

Most of the people who dealt with the customers were non-technical, so most of the information the circuit designers needed wasn't captured. The contact details of the people within the customer's organisation who could provide the information required, were also often missing. So there would be a series of conversations going backwards and forwards to the customer until the information was attained.

The bonus point encouraged sales teams to get orders 'on the books' as quickly as possible. Therefore, often orders were put on the system without all the relevant information. Sales would often use the excuse that they were 'not technical' for not having the information. But it was also apparent that some salespeople got their orders processed faster because they shouted loudest.

It was company policy that a signature accompanied every order, so faxes were used. Unfortunately no sample signatures were held by the company, so the signatures could not be verified. The order form had been based on another form from another earlier version of the company that had not sold circuits, hence the use of free text fields. It could be difficult to read people's writing and mistakes were made when this information was transferred into the order application.

At this stage the team was still forming, although they were storming as well. Once they had found someone whose 'fault' it was, the baggage came back out and the finger pointing began again. The body language was either very aggressive or defensive, depending on which side of the table the people were on.

It was important to show the whole team that it was not solely the fault of the Circuit Design team. When I suggested we just sack the Circuit Design team, the cheers filled the room. Then I pointed out that without them there would be no circuits and ultimately no business, so they would all be out of a job.

Slowly some started to realise that they had a direct impact on circuit design, but not all of them, so I needed to establish this and used what I call my '3-Why' theory.

The '3-Why' theory is that if you ask someone why they do a job three times you might get a realistic answer or the person is likely to end up confused. This is because the 3-why sessions usually follow a particular pattern:

The first time you ask why someone does a particular job, the most common response is that they will tell you how long they have done it for:

Analyst – 'Why do you do that?'

SME – 'I've done this for the last five years, that's why I'm the subject matter expert.'

I pointed out that that might be true, but that's how long they have done it for, not why they do it.

The second time you ask 'why', the most common response is that they will tell you it was how they were shown:

Analyst – 'Why do you do that?'

SME – 'It was the way that I was shown to do it.'

I pointed out that was how they did it, not why they did it.

Around the room people were starting to understand the question. In fact what I was asking was, 'What is the operational justification for the tasks you carry out and the impact of these tasks on the end-to-end process?'

Another clue is when the group understand this question, you will see that a number of them will not make eye contact, in case you ask them why they do what they do. It started to became apparent very quickly that very few, if any of them, had ever questioned the impact their role had on the end-to-end process, or what they did within the order process. This can have quite an impact on members of staff who have been in a company for a number of years and never questioned why they did what they did.

The third time you ask 'why' you will either get a justification in terms of the impact on the end-to-end process, or more commonly, 'I don't know why I do it.'

There are various methodologies that endeavour to establish the 'value' of each individual step in the end-to-end process. The principal idea is that if you are doing a step that adds no value, why do it?

This is one of the tipping points in the development of the team. They had finished storming. They collectively started to realise that they were all contributors to the end-to-end process and therefore all had a responsibility to the end-to-end process and that their actions directly or indirectly affected other parts of the company.

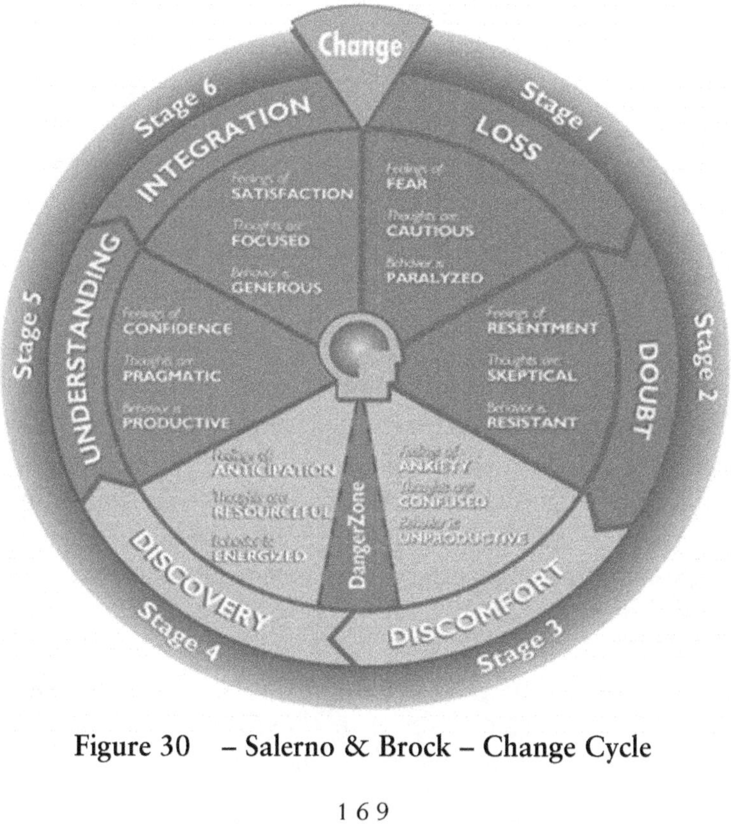

Figure 30 – Salerno & Brock – Change Cycle

There is a very good book written by Ann Salerno and Lillie Brock called 'The Change Cycle', which the publisher describes as a book that, 'offers a clear, powerful, well-developed, and easy-to-understand model for predicting people's behaviours, thoughts, and feelings in organisational change'.

The book takes the reader through six stages a person will go through during a change programme, and the people in this team were no different. They had reached the 'Danger Zone', the point where either they would move forward or stall and fall backwards.

They were outside of their comfort zone. They had started to map processes and the scenarios that made up the processes. They had only mapped a few processes, yet it had taken them weeks to gather all of the information and get that information verified by their own departments to ensure they had captured all the accurate information in the 'As Is' maps.

The size of the task seemed too daunting. There was simply too much to do, this why they were in this danger zone.

There is a well-used phrase, 'How does one eat an elephant?'

The answer is, 'One bite at a time', and the same was true here. Just because there was a lot to do didn't change the approach, what it did do was give the team a method of articulating to the senior management the amount of work this programme was going to take. It gave the senior management the opportunity to decide whether they would increase the timescales originally forecast for this part of the programme, or focus on a smaller number of processes.

The Einstein quote, 'The significant problems we face cannot be solved at the same level of thinking we were at when we created them'" was true. The team members were now beginning to change their level of thinking, as was the management team. All of them were moving up the business process capability maturity model, because they were getting to the stage where they could set realistic expectations of how long things were going to take to do, rather than guessing.

The body language within the team also started to change. They would greet each other with more open gestures, sometimes even physical contact of arm touches, pats or hugs and, as the Christmas period came and went, kisses were exchanged. Another measure I often use to map the progress of a team is the level of banter that flies around a room. To begin with people are either polite or hostile depending on who they feel they are defending or attacking, but as they get to know each other as people, these barriers start to dissolve and people start to have a laugh and a joke with each other.

They remapped the process again, but this time instead of doing it to see whose fault it was, they were mapping the process to see how they could collectively find a solution. Their language was starting to change. Whereas earlier someone might say, 'I can't do this because you/they don't do...', they were now saying, 'To be able to do this, I need...' And listing their needs.

Other members of the team would volunteer, 'I can get you that piece of information.' Their language was becoming more supportive and less blaming.

They were ready to move to the next stage.

11.6 Create Solution

The team was as much a part of the final solution as the changes to the processes, applications and systems, and therefore they had to be changed in their outlook of themselves.

This is vital before the team could move to the stage of creating the solution. They had to be working as a team and that wouldn’t have happened if they were still in their blame culture and still at each other’s throats.

We had an agreement that everyone signed up to:

‘There is no such thing as a bad idea, only a better one.’

Therefore, everyone’s voice was heard, no-one was more important than anyone else. Every contribution was valued. The members of the team stopped seeing the people round the table as ‘Finance’ or ‘IT’ or ‘HR’, they were ‘Steve’, ‘Peter’ and ‘Jan’.

The first step in this process of change was to give the team a name. A name that was outside of their silo identity, a name that made them think of themselves as part of this team. They decided to call themselves ‘Change Champions’. The name itself is less important than the process of collectively choosing a name. It is the giving each of them another identity that is important.

Then the solution programme needed a name. This is key to getting over some of the resistance to change described earlier, because it gives the programme an identity that senior management can communicate to the whole company. As the setting of customers’ expectations had been the driving force behind the project, the team came up with the name **MORSE**, from **M**eeting **O**u**R** Customer**S’** **E**xpectations.

The name caused a lot of amusement, a man with a large magnifying glass was on top of all the emails and reports, the theme tune from the television series ‘Inspector Morse’ accompanied programme presentations. To some this may seem an almost childish approach, but this is a serious step. The identity of a programme will ensure that people cannot use the excuse they didn't know about it. If staff have to admit they know about it, then they have to admit that they know the profile the programme has, the products or projects it is trying to achieve, and how important the senior management have said it ranks against other projects that will be running in parallel with it.

The programme identity also assists in heading up the communications plan. The regular monthly updates on change products, which would be top & tailed by the senior management sponsor.

The solution they came up with had four initial change products to it:

- A PC for each team member
- Collection of accurate and relevant data only once
- Pre-sales support for a non-technical Sales force
- Changes to terms and conditions

Firstly, each member of the team in Circuit Design needed their own PC, but there was a ban on IT purchase. The IT member of the team solved this problem for us. It is my experience that few organisations fully exploit all the IT they buy. This is more prevalent in some public sector organisations than in the private sector. Budgets run in parallel with annual tax years. Certain departments will see their funding cut if they don't spend all their allocated money in a particular year, so at the back end of the financial year there is a lot of spending. IT, by its very nature, takes a lot of funding. It is often the backbone of most organisations and they simply could not operate without it, it is therefore understandable that a lot of funding is spent on new IT. However, it usually can't all be installed in one go. The resource requirements outweigh the finite resource the IT department has at its disposal. Therefore, PCs may be purchased, but are stored.

It is also my experience that IT subject matter experts can always lay their hands on IT that is not being used. In this manner we managed to get PCs for the engineers who didn't have any. The first product had been delivered at no additional cost to the organisation.

Most staff and customers would not have noticed this change, as there was a large backlog that had to be sorted out initially. This was another reason that the communications plan did not inform staff that the additional PCs had been acquired and installed, until staff started to notice an increase in throughput. In this way the change programme got some good press for the delivery of a product and the organisation had quantifiable evidence that the programme was delivering benefit to the organisation.

The second product was the collection of data the Circuit Design Engineers required and the access to that data. Rather than retyping information from faxes, it made more sense to collect all the relevant information that was required in one go and have one 'single version of the truth' that was then shared by everybody, rather than each department having its own populated database. Many applications use this 'single version of the truth' as one of their primary building principles, because it doesn't make any sense to repeat the collection of data that another part of the organisation has already collected, and unfortunately demonstrates to the customer that an organisation's internal processes do not communicate with each other. This is bound to have a negative impact on the customer experience and how customers view the organisation.

There are occasions where restricted access to a person's information is perfectly valid. This may be for personal, professional or confidentiality reasons. However, in this case there was little or no reason for restricted access to the order. Yet previously, getting access to this information was very difficult. People get very protective of information in their control. The phrase 'Knowledge is power' unfortunately is often believed. People will, for their own ends, ensure that they alone hold a piece of information under the often misapprehension that this will make them immune to dismissal or redundancy.

Many years ago when I was a Technical Apprentice, a colleague resigned quoting that he was 'irreplaceable' and that the organisation would collapse without him. Another colleague said something to me that I have never forgot. 'If you think you are irreplaceable, fill a bucket with water and push your clenched fist into the water for thirty seconds. Then remove your fist and wait for a minute to pass. Then look into the bucket and the hole in the water is how much you'll be missed.' In business no-one is irreplaceable.

Yet this non-sharing of data is often rife in organisations where there is blame culture, silo mentality, a lack of cross-functional communication and so on.

One of the major cultural leaps forward this team had made was to give up this particular 'sack of baggage'. Read-only access to the order application was given to the Circuit Design team. This enabled them to 'copy and paste' all the information they required into their own application without any retyping.

Of course this would only be of real value if the right data was being collected in the first place. This led to the third product.

The third product needed to overcome the fact that the sales team were not technical. It was agreed that when a sales lead got to the 70% stage of the sales funnel, a technical person would be assigned to the order. For those of you who do not have experience of a sales process, in its broadest terms, at the top of the funnel are many prospects, however when they are at the top of the funnel the chance of closing the order is low. As the prospects move through the funnel they will grow fewer in number, but the chance of closing the deal grows. When it reached the 70% mark that meant we, as a company, were in the last two bidding for this piece of business.

The nominating of a technical support was seen favourably by clients as a very professional approach to ensure we could meet the expectations that we set. The Technical support would have a meeting or series of meetings with the internal customer technical support to ensure that all the correct information was collected. There was the risk that if we were not successful in winning the bid the time would have been wasted, but it was vital in hitting the timescales in the bids that were won so this became an acceptable risk.

The fourth product was a process change that was to engage the sales force in a way they had not been engaged before. The Sales subject matter expert put it very simply, 'If you want the sales people interested in the end-to-end process, then you have to move the point at which they get their bonus from the start of the order process to the end of the order process.' An easy statement to say, and no doubt true, but difficult to introduce.

There were many occasions early on in the team building process and mapping and analysis stages when the subject matter expert from HR questioned her involvement in the team. She had initially said at the first meeting that she thought she was obviously in the wrong meeting because this had nothing to do with HR. I assured her she would be vital to the creation of the solution, and therefore, needed to be part of the team and in from the beginning. I had deliberately sat next to her when I knew the sales SME was going to announce the statement above. I asked her, 'How do we change the terms and conditions of the sales people so the bonus point moves to the end of the process?'" Her smile was all I needed to let me know that now she understood why we needed her.

Of course senior management buy-in was going to be crucial at this stage. This was not something that would be greeted with any applause. It reinforced the commitment of the senior management. Changes to terms and conditions didn't end with the sales people. It had been established that the current bonus system was based on the silo key performance indicators that did not reflect the end-to-end process and therefore the actual service being delivered. Therefore, this structure was also changed to reflect the end-to-end service.

Now they had their solution, they could implement it.

11.7 Implement Solution

The first four products the programme would deliver as the solution had now been agreed. Now they had to be implemented.

I have mentioned on numerous occasions in this book that one of the most critical things is communication and it is vital when letting people know what is going to change and how those changes are going to affect them as individuals

There were the practicalities of introduction of changes in parallel with all the other programmes that were also running. Like all other organisations, there were a number of projects running that were at various stages. The solution products had to be introduced via formal change control and testing.

Not all organisations have a formal change control process in place. Departments are allowed to change things in a largely unstructured manner. IT is often involved as changes can often include either new hardware or software, so it is in the IT department's best interests to have some form of change control. Initially this might be very ad hoc, but it would be my recommendation that something more formal is put in place. This does not have to be over-complex, simply recording the requested changes on a spreadsheet so IT Engineers can book their time to proactive change requests as opposed to reactive fault calls would be a good start. At least in that way an organisation will start to get a feel for the volume of changes that happen on a regular basis.

Fortunately the business had already seen the potential benefit of having co-ordinated change and had set up a unit that was responsible for the introduction of changes. This unit worked very closely with the MORSE change team, as the Change Unit had adopted the use of the processes that had already been mapped and built into a Business Operations Model. The main advantage of having such a model was that when any change request was raised, from a simple change to a project, the unit had introduced a field on the change request form that asked the question, 'Which business processes will this change affect?' Then they would be aware from the earliest possible moment whether there would be a conflict between change requests.

11.8 Exercise 2 – Change Conflicts

This is a very simple exercise. I would challenge you to find the mechanism your organisation currently uses to ensure that when two or more projects are attempting to change the same process, but to do different things, the first time you find this out isn't when they both go live and the process stops working.

The use of the business operations model ensures that at the project initiation stage, the project manager has to state which business processes are to be affected by this project. The change team can then very easily see whether more than one parallel project plans to affect the same process and can easily get the various project managers together – either by voice conference or in person – to 'find out' what they are trying to achieve. That way potential conflicts within the process can be resolved or escalated, even before work on the project has begun.

If the result of this exercise is that you cannot find such a mechanism within your organisation, I'd ask the IT Director, Operations Director and a few board level people, why not?

The model was a simple Excel spreadsheet, see fig 31 below.

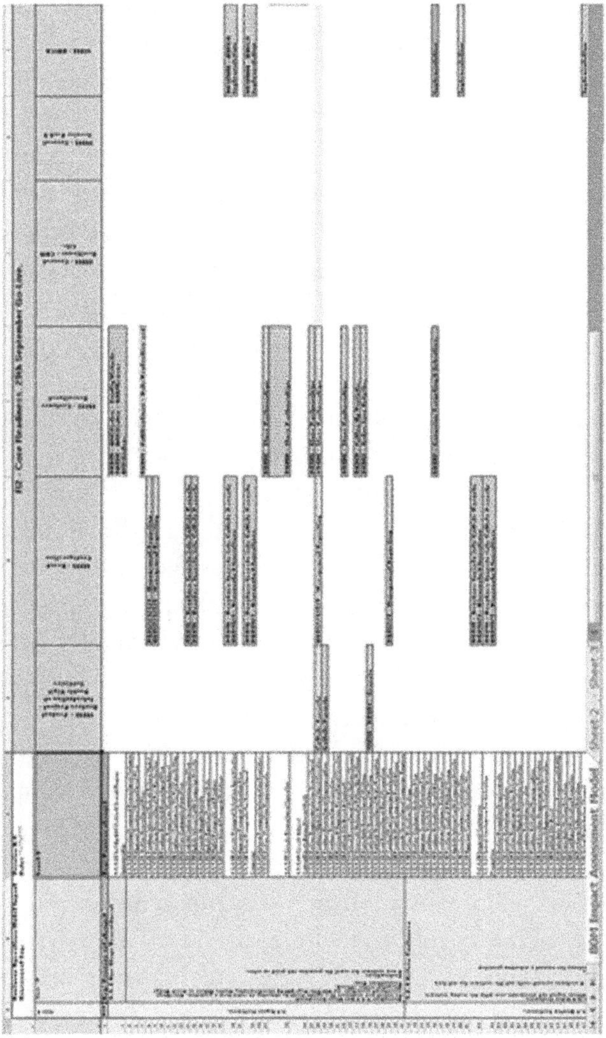

Figure 31 – Business Operations Model

The first three columns of the spreadsheet are levels one, two and three of the business operations model. Within column three are the references to each of the process maps already drawn, and these were held in another drawing application that could export out Excel, so this spreadsheet could be updated whenever something went live. The remaining columns are the individual projects, split into the phases of when they would go live. Where there was no impact on the business processes, the cells have been left blank. Where there was impact on the business process, the cell is shaded and the impact was detailed.

The main advantage of having the information on a simple spreadsheet was that it was very simple to see whether more than one project would impact the same part of the process model. The IT requirements for the different projects might not in themselves appear to negatively impact each other, however, if by its introduction the two projects were trying to get the processes working in different ways then this could be identified early rather than not realising there could be a problem until after go live.

Of course the implementation also includes communicating to the people affected by the change, and this might not be easy. In this example the re-engineered process would require one department to collect all the information the process needed at the start of the process, enabling this 'single version of the truth' to be used by the whole process

The Subject Matter Expert was the person who would communicate this message back to the department but it was not going to be an easy job. I often recommend to subject matter experts that they will need to grow at least two more layers of skin, because they will need to be 'thick-skinned' to stand up and sell a message that an audience does not want to hear.

The audience was told the whole story of the analysis and how it made sense to collect all the information only once. While some might have followed the logic and reasoning, they all came to the same conclusion that this department was being asked to do more work and would not be giving any more staff to do it.

Then one member of the audience, who I describe as the 'Doom Merchant', spoke up.

Every organisation has what I call 'Doom Merchants'; they are people who are always negative, 'It won't work' is their usual reaction to any suggested change. They have an automatic resistance to change because, although they complain a lot, they like the world the shape it is and don't want it changed. I often describe these people as those walking about wearing a sandwich board stating 'the end is nigh'.

And as soon as the presentation was finished their first question was, 'What's in it for us?' This is not an unreasonable question from their perspective but, when the Subject Matter Expert answered, 'The company as a whole becomes more efficient', the response was, 'So what?'

This negative reaction is – to an extent – understandable, because from the perspective of that individual department there is no tangible benefit. There is nothing 'in it' for them as individuals, other than their impact on other departments. This is why it is ***key*** for the subject matter experts to do this presentation. If an external consultant delivers this presentation, the reaction will be that he or she doesn't know what they are talking about because they are 'not from here'. If the presentation is delivered by a senior manager, it will be seen as a change that is being imposed and that will cause its own resistance. It has to be one of their own, because that person will have a level of credibility nobody else could have.

It doesn't make the presentation any easier, but the fact that we had decided early on that the subject matter experts would deliver this part of the communication plan meant we could prepare for it.

I call this the 'double glazing salesman technique' and, with all due respect to double glazing sales people, it is a technique using a series of closed questions where the sales person has already worked out in advance what your objections will be and has an answer for all your objections. The purpose of this is to lead the client to a position where there is no reason why you should not have whatever they are selling.

To prepare the Subject Matter Experts, we would role play the presentation, not only to allow the subject matter experts the opportunity to hone those skills, but also to flush out what we thought would be the likely negative questions and ensure we had answers for them.

Then when the Subject Matter Expert presented back to their team, they had the answers to most, if not all, of the questions they were going to face. They would list on a flip chart the reasons the Doom Merchant gave that it would not work, then for each of these reasons they would ask, 'but if that was overcome, would it work?' This would continue until the Doom Merchant ran out of ideas, which they do eventually. The Subject Matter Expert could then conclude by saying to the whole group, but really aimed at the Doom Merchant, 'So if these things were sorted, it would work?'

The answer they were looking for was level of agreement, even a reluctant one. Hopefully the Doom Merchant will add, 'But you'll never get those things sorted, so it won't work.'

The Subject Matter Expert can then go through each of the things listed on the flip chart describing how each has been addressed, ending with the previously agreed statement that if these things were 'overcome' the solution should work.

This is not the only way these sessions could be or should be conducted, and every organisation is different so the subject matter experts will know how best to communicate the messages back to their own areas of the business. I am stating that preparation is vital to this stage of the programme. The solutions will need to be 'sold' back to the teams the subject matter experts came from, particularly those who will be impacted in a way that could be interpreted as negative from those departments.

This is one of the reasons that if it is possible early in the life of the programme to deliver 'products' which make life easier for some people, this should be done and communicated well around the organisation. It will help the profile of the team delivering the programme and will mean that when it comes time to deliver difficult messages, their credibility has already been established as a team that delivers things that are good for the company end-to-end.

At a conference I attended in 2009 it was stated that a timescale of seven to twelve weeks is the window in which the first tangible benefit has to be delivered to the organisation, or the programme will lose both momentum and credibility. I concur with this recommendation. I would recommend a workshop early on in the programme that looks solely at 'Points of pain' across the organisation. What really gets staff seething about the current organisation? Whatever comes out of this session should be investigated to see if there is one of these 'points of pain' that can be solved by the introduction of a change product, even if it is only the first version. In this way the momentum of the programme will be maintained and the fact that it is delivering positive benefit will ultimately make more difficult changes easier to sell.

If an organisation believes there is a lot of apathy or non-vocal refusal resistance, as previous change programmes have not been successful, it might be better to deliver a number of products without a lot of communication to sow the seeds of success. So when a few milestones have already been hit, the communications plan can kick into action and the things already achieved can be listed as parts of the change programme. If staff have already seen benefits from these products it will stir some people out of apathy and may make some of the non-verbal refusal types reconsider.

Momentum is really the key. The delivery of change products, particularly ones that address issues across an organisation that have been 'bones of contention', will give the change programme a reputation that 'it delivers'. Some of the apathy that would have looked at it as simply 'another initiative that will fail like all the others before', will fade. People will start to believe that things are achievable. As mentioned earlier, this is how to get people past the Salerno and Brock 'Danger Zone'.

So, with all the right building blocks now in place, it was time to implement. As stated, all the new products would go through a period of 'testing' prior to go-live.

11.9 Outcomes

In terms of the enterprise architecture, there weren't too many changes. The end-to-end process still broadly went through the same stages. There had been changes, for example, in the sales stage when technical staff would be involved to ensure the correct information was gathered, but the process was the same.

The applications used had not been changed greatly. The initial capture screens had additional fields to ensure that all the technical data could be collected. Therefore fields had been added to the forms at the front end of the process but, as these were filled in by the technical staff in pre-sales, it didn't make a huge impact to the department collecting the data.

The systems had not been changed at all. The Circuit Design technical staff needed a PC each, but the configuration of the platforms used had not changed. There were no changes in the network, in fact the loading on the network was lower than before as, instead of large Excel spreadsheet being posted from person to person, the order forms were held in a central location and staff just updated their part of the form in their part of the process then emailed a message to the next stage stating that the work had been carried out.

Roles and responsibilities had changed. The Technical staff were responsible for getting the right information at the meeting with the client. The Sales staff were responsible for ensuring that all relevant information was gathered before orders were submitted. The bonus scheme for all staff had changed.

Indirectly all of their roles had changed, as they now had their new identity as Change Champions.

The largest changes were in the culture. The issues that had to be addressed were:

- A lack of Cross-Functional Communication
  - Staff don't know each other

- A lack of Cross-Functional Co-operation
    - Staff don't care about the rest of the company
- A lack of Understanding of the End-2-End Process
    - Staff only focused on their own silo
    - KPIs only within silo not end-2-end
- A lack of 'Ownership' of End-2-End Process
    - Senior Managers only want to be accountable for what they can control
    - Organisation structured in Silos
- Blame Culture – 'Whose Fault' when Customers complained
- Silo Mentality
- Political in-fighting
- Resistance to change

Issue – No cross-functional communication or co-operation. This silo mentality occurs in many organisations where the end-to-end processes have not been looked at. Directors only accept accountability and responsibility for things under their direct control and therefore anything that is not under their direct control is somebody else's problem. Staff didn't know or care about other departments.

Resolution – The team of subject matter experts, now known as change champions, were the cross-functional channel that ensured that the collection of information was not being duplicated. The team knew the end-to-end process better than anyone in the company.

Issue – No understanding of the end-to-end process. Without this understanding there is a risk that departments will endeavour to improve their own processes by making changes that benefit them, but are counterproductive to another department several steps further down the process. Therefore, although changes are made for what appears to be good business reasons, the impact on the overall process is minimal or the bottlenecks are simply moved to another part of the process and therefore to another part of the organisation. All the metrics were within individual silos, so all the attention was focused 'within silo'.

Resolution – now that the team had mapped the processes, they all understood the process in its entirety. The team made a series of suggestions that eventually changed the metrics that were collected to reflect how well the organisation meets the expectations it sets to customers. Members of the team transferred into the new Change Unit where their knowledge of the process was put to good use in the assessment of change requests. The knowledge of the process enabled the staff to have a good understanding of how changes would affect the process and, if they weren't sure, then they had the network to contact one of the other Change Champions to ask.

Issue – No ownership. If nobody owns a process then a number of things will happen. More than one party may try and change their part of the process, for what appears to be good business reasons, but subsequently these changes create a negative effect on another department further down the end-to-end process and, as a result, the end-to-end process becomes less efficient. Another result of no ownership is that if there are problems within a process that no-one owns, then everyone assumes it is someone else's responsibility to fix the problem, so nobody fixes it, or they don't question that something is wrong because 'we've always done this process like this', or 'this was how I was shown how to do this process'. Does any of those sound familiar?

Resolution – As mentioned earlier in the description of the 'New Starter' process, it is important for senior management to accept that they need to own the end-to-end processes. The resolution was for each end-to-end process to be given an owner at Director level. Each Director would only have direct control over a fraction of the process they owned, which by default meant that as a senior management team they had to start to work closer together because they became suppliers and customers of each other.

Issue – Blame culture. When organisations have a blame culture, they will spend a large amount of time witch hunting whose fault it is that something went wrong within a process. This is unproductive time which has a direct cost to the business. This then leads to a non-professional behaviour where parts of the organisation are deliberately being uncooperative with each other, orders are not given the correct priority because of personalities, baggage builds up and so on. The one who suffers the most from this is the customer. Although this behaviour can be seen as non-professional, it does exist and can be very divisive to the performance of an organisation.

Resolution – Once the team had gone through their Tuckman 'Forming' and 'Storming' phases and had realised that each of their departments had a direct impact on other parts of the business, they started moving from a 'Blame Culture' to a 'Support Culture'. A good sign for the team starting to change from one to the other is that the word 'they' is used less to describe other parts of the organisation. The language starts to change from 'it is their fault my department can't do this task because they don't give us the right information', to 'to do this task I need the following information.' When they moved towards the 'Support Culture' more team members would change their language from arguing why it was not their department's fault to, 'I can get you that information.'

From almost the first meeting the personalities started to show through. Very soon they started to look at each other as people not as the departments they represented.

This also had benefits for the business outside of the initial MORSE programme. Subsequently if a customer complained or an inefficiency was unearthed, the Change Champions would be called together to find out what had gone wrong and fix it. As soon as the issue was analysed people would put their hands up, 'That was my department's fault.' But there was no inquisition, no arguments. Their approach was an 'Ok, how do we fix it?' attitude.

From time to time additional members of staff were asked to join the team to solve a particular issue. The team themselves would see this new member enter the room with all their baggage, they would see them point the fingers of blame at whose fault it was that the issue had arisen in the first place. They would see how far they had grown as a team, because they could recognise all the negative aspects they themselves had displayed when they began the programme.

Issue – Resistance to change. (See section 11.2)

As mentioned, there were Doom Merchants and they would complain at every presentation that things 'wouldn't work' and that this programme was 'just stuff we've seen before and it didn't work last time so it's not going to work this time'. But some people in the same room would argue with the Doom Merchant pointing out the change products that had been delivered and the benefits that had come as a result. And some added that the Doom Merchant had said the 'world would end' and it hadn't. So although I don't believe you will ever fully silence the Doom Merchants, you can get to a point where the audience they command is greatly reduced and more people are brought into the continual change mentality and are therefore less resistant to change.

Then, as this programme was about 'Continual Improvement', it started again. The sticking to scope had created a large 'snag list' of 'unknown unknowns' that needed to be addressed, so change requests were raised and the cycle began again.

11.10 Conclusion

The outcome of this particular programme was that the number of orders which met customers' expectations went up from twelve per cent to sixty per cent within three months of the programme delivering the changes, with steady increases up to above eighty five per cent within six months.

The team had moved successfully from a blame culture to a support culture by working together. This collaboration had improved not only the process which was, after all, the reason for setting up the team, but had assisted in changing the entire way in which change was viewed within the company. The organisation had moved through the various stages of the business process capability maturity model. As described in part one of this book, the jump from 'defined' to 'optimised' is best described as the change in culture from where change is seen as a series of 'one-off' projects, to a point where the culture within the organisation is one of continual improvement and change is seen as the 'norm'.

If organisations do not see change as the norm then they are not at the 'optimised' stage. As a result of this, they will not reach the stage where they could be independent of external expertise. Therefore they will always have to use expensive external resource to try and change them and will continue just changing single parts of the enterprise architecture and, to use the baby learning to run analogy, they will continue to put new running shoes on the baby and be surprised that it still cannot run.

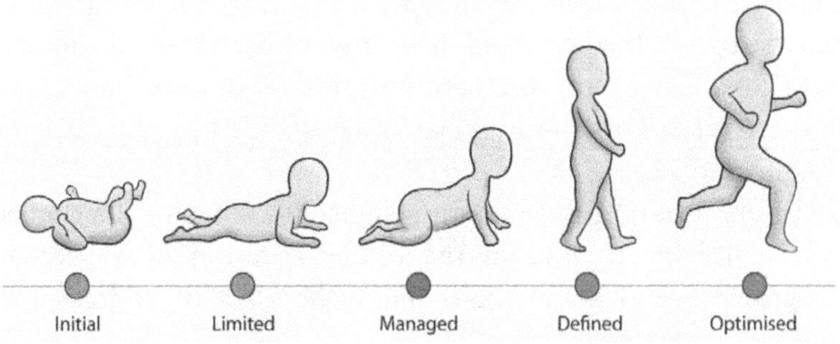

Figure 2 – Business Process Capability Maturity Model

Culture is often seen as an afterthought and that is why I describe it as the forgotten variable. Yet as you can see from this case study, its impact is huge and this change programme would not have worked without the changes to culture.

In a Business Process Management Masterclass I created and run, I put up a slide with this information as the cultural issues that need to be addressed:

- A lack of Cross-Functional Communication

- Staff don't know each other
- A lack of Cross-Functional Co-operation
  - Staff don't care about the rest of the company
- A lack of Understanding of the End-2-End Process
  - Staff only focused on their own silo
  - KPIs only within silo not end-2-end
- A lack of 'Ownership' of End-2-End Process
  - Senior Managers only want to be accountable for what they can control
  - Organisation structured in Silos
- Blame Culture – 'Whose Fault' when customers complained
- Silo Mentality
- Political in-fighting
- Resistance to change

Delegates from public sector, private sector, UK companies, European and further afield, have always been able to identify with this. Therefore, these are universal issues not limited to just one type of organisation, so I suggest that will include your organisation.

I hope I have given you an insight into some of the things you will have to face in the implementation of a change programme and some tools and techniques to address the issues you may face.

It is my belief and experience that enthusiasm can be as infectious as apathy and is an excellent force to combat apathy. But this needs to be tempered with patience; you will not change the whole organisation overnight. So you need to be selective. Choose your products carefully, go for points of pain if you can to gain early momentum. Only set expectations you are confident you can meet. Single out and silence your Doom Merchants.

Ensure there is the management buy-in, as demonstrated in the section on resistance to change (Section 11.2); this is key to the removal of most of the types of resistance. Make sure the subject matter experts are available and if you don't have the Business Analyst skills in-house, ensure the programme gets external expertise. This again stresses how imperative senior management buy-in is to a successful change programme. They won't be involved in the detail, but they have the responsibility to ensure that blockers are removed and the team is supported.

I run a half-day session for senior management, sometimes to kick off a change programme, sometimes to take them through the stages of a change programme and how it will affect their organisation, if they haven't done one before. I will ask them outright if they are serious about it. Invariably everyone says that they are, but I reiterate, 'Are you really serious? Because if you're not, you're wasting my time and your money, so are you really serious?' When they again state that they are, I tell them that they have given me their 'Really Serious Mandate', and that I will wave it in front of them on the occasions when the buy-in and commitment gets put to the test.

Quite often the first time this happens is in the selection of the subject matter experts. When I ask for a one hour meeting with their superstars, I can often get them. When I go back later and say that I need the same people full-time for the next three months, lots of excuses around themes like, 'we have a business to run', or, 'the world won't just stop so you can get off and run this programme', or, 'this isn't the only important thing we're doing in the business', will all come from them. To this I ask, 'So you're not really serious then?' This discussion can and does happen on a number of occasions, and these discussions can be heated as the senior management team will have many difficult decisions to make and will have a great number of challenges they have to overcome in addition to the change programme. But this is where their commitment will be tested and studies by Gartner and the like have shown the ones who can stick to that commitment and support the change team, even through difficult times, are the ones that achieve the most.

If you can identify that you are at the bottom end of the

business process capability maturity model, that's not a failure, it's a great success, because there are many organisations who don't know where they are on that learning curve. At least you will know. At the first three stages I would recommend getting external expertise, at those stages it would be unfair and unwise to 'assume' your people will be able to just 'sort it out', but I would recommend external experts who are good at skills transfer, so that as you rise through the stages you will become less reliant on them, and you and they are comfortable with this progression.

Take a dollop of determination, a large order of common sense, a side order of intelligence and a sprinkling of humour and many things are possible.

Good luck!

David

12 Exercises

Both of the following exercises will assist you in determining where your organisation is currently on the business process capability maturity model.

If an organisation is near the upper end of the model, then you will find positive results from both of these exercises. If, on the other hand, you do not find positive results from either or both of these fairly simple exercises, then you have some evidence to take to your senior management that something is definitely wrong in your organisation. And if these things are not addressed then things like benefits realisation, efficiencies and effectiveness in changes will be at best limited, and at worst will cost money and won't really deliver much in the way of long-term benefit.

The analogy used earlier in this book looked at the development of a baby from lying on its back kicking its legs and arms about, through flipping onto its front, crawling, walking and finally learning to run. When organisations are at the bottom end of the maturity model and simply replace a piece of software assuming that the organisation 'will sort itself out', this is like putting an expensive pair of running shoes on a baby that is still lying on its back kicking its legs about and expecting it to be able to run. If an organisation does not have the experience and cross-functional co-ordination to manage change to cross-functional processes, they have as much chance of success as the baby does, and should not be surprised when they do not get the outcome they wished for.

Hopefully these exercises will give you the evidence to make your senor management think again.

12.1 Exercise 1

The object of exercise one is to demonstrate the level of cross-functional co-operation and end-to-end process ownership within your organisation

The most common process in every organisation, whether it is commercial or public sector, is the new starter process. And if you are in a job, or have ever been in a job, then you have experience of being through this process.

In an organisation that is at the 'optimised' or top end of the business process capability maturity model, when a new starter comes into work on their first day they will have the contents of the following checklist available.

Items Required	Items available
1 - A fixed desk, hot-desk or some place to work	Yes / No
2 - A personal computer or laptop	Yes / No
3 - A telephone (either fixed or mobile)	Yes / No
4 - All the applications you require for your role are loaded onto the PC or laptop you receive	Yes / No
5 - You have user names and passwords to grant you access to all the corporate applications you require to carry out the role	Yes / No
6 - You have meetings set into your diary with key individuals to explain what the organisation is doing, your role within it, and what is expected of you in the short, medium and longer terms.	Yes / No

Figure 32 – New Starter Exercise

Using the list above, how many things could you answer yes to? One, two, three perhaps, maybe none?

Ask your HR department:

1. Where does the new starter process begin?
2. Which senior manager/director/VP owns the end-to-end process?

Then ask the Finance department, the IT department and the Operations department the same two questions. If the answer to question 2 is a consistent 'nobody', then you probably didn't answer 'Yes' to all six items.

You may use the components table in appendix one to ask further questions or gather information.

Often individual managers will take ownership and drive the process for new starters in their own departments, particularly if they have been through an awful experience themselves, but the only way to have a proper solution is to have a formal end-to-end owned process.

A working process should look something like the one on the following page. How close is yours? For costing, see section 6.6.

12.2 Exercise 2

The object of exercise two is to demonstrate whether your organisation has a mechanism in place for ensuring that two or more projects aren't trying to change the same process but in different ways.

If your organisation has begun to manage its processes, then a number of process maps will have been drawn. These may have started out as large pieces of brown wrapping paper covered in Post-it notes, and incidentally there is nothing wrong with this method capture. However, at some stage the information will need to be transferred to some application.

Most organisations using Microsoft as their base application will have Visio, which is okay for recording process steps, however it has limitations as it wasn't initially designed as a process capture tool.

There are a huge variety of tools on the market, matching every budget, but for this exercise you need to consider how these

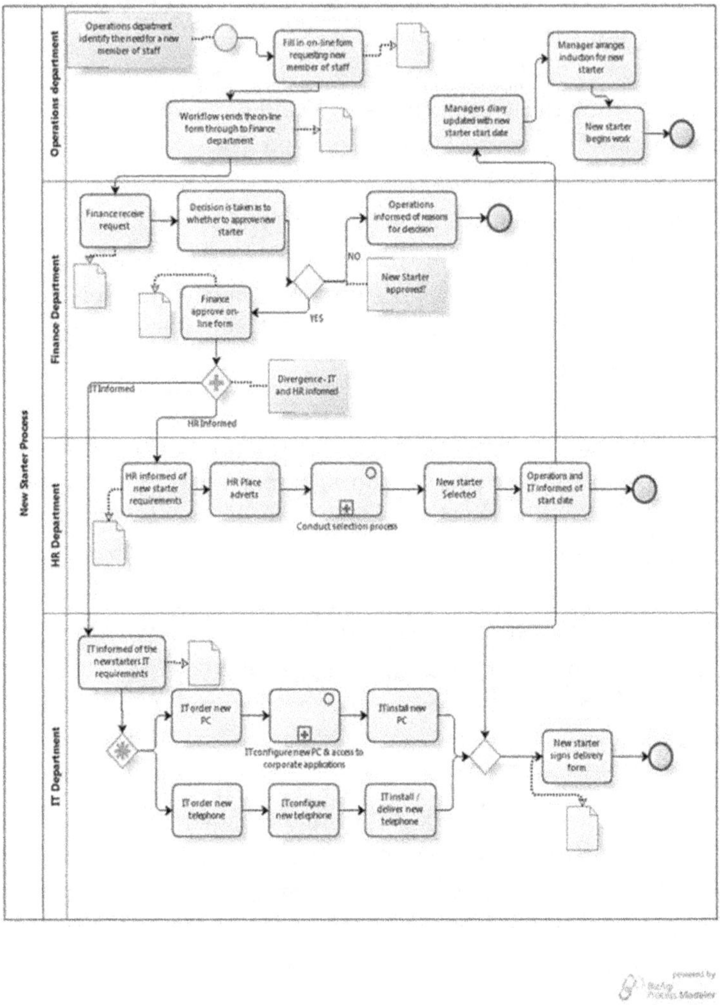

Figure 33 – BPMN – New Starter Process

process maps are stored and what reference model is used for their archiving.

If your organisation doesn't have a process archive, then your organisation has already failed this exercise. The same form in appendix one can be used to gather information.

If your organisation does have an archive for processes and does have a formal change management policy, then that would be the place to start. I'd ask IT first, as most IT departments will have some form of change management policy. It might be ITIL compliant, it might be more ad-hoc, but at least it's somewhere to start.

Ask the questions:

1. How do we avoid two or more projects trying to change the same business process in different ways?
2. Who owns 'Change Management' within our organisation in terms of change requests being managed end-to-end? This would include non-IT-related changes, for example to business processes.
3. At what stage in the project management cycle does the question get asked that would ascertain whether the change request was trying to change a business process?
4. Following question 3, who owns checking whether any other projects are also trying to change the same business process?

If you don't get positive answers to these questions, sooner or later two or more projects will go-live and the process, which was working previously, will stop working. It may get covered up under the title of 'teething problems with the new system', or the new application will have to be 'backed out' until the process issues are resolved.

Or, maybe it has already happened in your organisation, in which case you should have all the evidence to present to your senior management team the cost of doing it wrong.

Good Hunting!

13 Appendices

The following pages are appendices that can be used to assist your change programme.

The first appendix is my Business Process Components table. This is really a checklist that can be used at programme set-up to see the amount of information that an organisation currently holds about its processes. This can be a powerful tool in demonstrating to senior management how little they know about their own organisation, or how much information is currently stored in people's heads.

The information listed in the components list should be stored in a single environment. This might be an existing business process management application, but just an area on a server is fine for starters if nothing currently exists, using each section as sub-folders for each process.

1. Process Flows. This section will assist in gathering all existing diagrams, if they exist. It will assist in asking the questions to see what governance is currently in place and whether that governance is easy to find for any given process. It will establish whether anyone has seriously ever looked at all the scenarios that affect the day-to-day operation of an organisation.
2. Paperwork Flows. Many organisations are still heavily paper-based. The paperless office is still a very long way away for most organisations. People like paper, it's tangible, it won't freeze or crash like a PC can. The new term is 'Paper-lite' as some form of aspiration to remove some of the paper. It is at least a start. This section looks at

the number of forms that are used, who uses them, where they go, who owns them and how often they are reviewed to see if they are still relevant for the organisation.

3. Process Timings. When trying to ascertain gaps or bottlenecks/constraints in a process, a good understanding of its timings is required. How often is the process run? How long does it take? How long should it take? What would be an unacceptable time threshold for it to take? Are there known areas of bottlenecks? If there are, do these areas run at as close to 100% of their capacity? Follow a process so that cumulative and sequential timings can be established. This might lead to the cumulative parts of the process being focused on to make it faster without initially doing anything to the sequential process steps.
4. Interdependencies. This section covers the collection of all the triggers in and out of the process. This will assist in establishing the potential impact to other processes, roles, external parties, etc, when changes are suggested.
5. Data. This section covers all the aspects of data and can be very useful for flushing out where different parts of an organisation use a term that means different things. Never be afraid of asking, 'What does that mean?' I often ask people to explain to me what they do as though I was a child, or I reserve the right to ask what might be seen as a really silly question, because I don't understand the process. There have been many occasions when I ask, 'what does that mean?' and people either have real difficulty in actually explaining what it is or they don't know themselves and have reached a point where they would be too embarrassed to admit they don't know what it means.
6. Functional requirements. This section covers the way data currently flows from application to application, where that data is stored and backed up. What sort of security is in place? What sort of testing standards are in place? It covers the applications the roles involved in the process will need

to have access to so that they are able to carry out their roles.

7. Reporting. This section covers how the process is measured, who these reports go to and what types of decisions will be made as a result of them. There is a term DRIP which stands for Data-Rich-Information-Poor. Many organisations produce reams and reams of reports. But if it takes too long to go through them, then they are not adding value to the decision-making process and therefore are not adding value to the organisation. Ask yourself this question, 'If you are not going to make a decision as a result of something you see in a report, why are you reading it?' This section also covers who these reports go to and how often.
8. Roles & Responsibilities. This covers the roles that are included in the process. How are they measured, incentives and rewards given? What do they do? What skills do they need to be able to carry out the role?

So you can see, it is quite a large shopping list of information. However, if an organisation can easily lay its hands on the information requested in this components list then they have a really good understanding of their processes and will be able to make changes to those processes with the least risk of a negative impact to their organisation's day-to-day activities.

The second appendix is an extract from 'An early start to testing: how to test requirements' by Suzanne Robertson. This is a marvellous checklist if an organisation does not have a robust test management suite.

The third appendix is a simple timeline analyse spreadsheet that can be used if you want to carry out a simple exercise to establish some of the cost of delivery and where some people's time is eaten up. It should not be used or seen as a 'Big Brother' type of surveillance. There will be times during the day where people are standing at the coffee machine just chatting and catching up on office gossip. This might not be seen as particularly productive time, but many good business ideas have been hatched round a coffee machine.

13.1 Appendix 1 – Business Process Components

Business Process Definition	Business Process Deliverable	Tick [v] where the contents currently exist and are easy to find
1.Business Process Flows	1.1 Business Process Flow	
	1.2 Business Governance	
	1.3 Scenarios & Variations	
	By Organisational Hierarchy	
	By Operational Hierarchy.	
	By External Party.	
	1.4 Archiving Governance (including access to B.O.M to evaluate multiple change projects)	
2. Paperwork Flows	2.1 Forms Required (forms owned, under version control and periodically reviewed)	
3. Process Timings	3.1 Frequency of Process	
	(Ad Hoc and Regular)	
	3.2 Forecast Bottlenecks	
	3.3 Sequential and Cumulative Timings	
4. Interdependencies	4.1 Role Definition	
	4.2 Locations/Departments	
	4.3 External Parties	

	4.4 Systems	
	4.5 Authorisations/Approvals	
5. Data	5.1 Entity Models (if avail)	
	5.2 Data Dictionary	
	5.3 Data Transformation including conversion requirements if required	
6. Functional System Requirements	6.1 Functional Flows	
	6.2 Menu Security	
	6.3 Standard Testing Pack (Inc CIT – SIT UAT Alpha – Beta – Delta)	
	6.4 Operational Proving scripts/volumes, etc	
7. Reporting Requirements	7.1 Operational Reporting Requirements	
	7.2 Analytical Reporting Requirements –Top & Bottom 5	
	7.3 Exception Reporting Requirements	
8. Roles & Responsibilities	8.1 High Level Definition	
	8.2 Core Skills/Security Clearance, etc	
	8.3 Organisational Hierarchy (for escalations)	

1.3 Appendix 3 – Timeline Analysis Spreadsheet.

Timeline Analysis for				Employee Name										
Client Name														
Human Resources														
Start Date			14-Feb		End Date		28-Feb							
			Monday	Tuesday	Wednesday	Thursday	Friday	Monday	Tuesday	Wednesday	Thursday	Friday	Monday	Tuesday
08:30														
08:45			Opened Mail	Opened Mail	Opened Mail	Opened Mail	Opened Mail	Opened Mail	Opened Mail	Opened Mail	Opened Mail	Opened Mail	Opened Mail	Opened Mail
09:00														
09:15														
09:30														
09:45														
10:00														
10:15														
10:30														
10:45														
11:00														
11:15														
11:30														
11:45														
12:00														
12:15														
12:30														
12:45														
13:00														
13:15														
13:30														
13:45														
14:00														
14:15														
14:30														
14:45														
15:00														
15:15														
15:30														
15:45														
16:00														
16:15														
16:30														
16:45														
17:00														
17:15														
17:30														
17:45														
18:00														
18:15														
18:30														
18:45														
19:00														

1.2 Appendix 2 – Testing

Extract from 'An early start to testing: how to test requirements' by Suzanne Robertson.

Testing.

Every piece of new technology needs to be tested before it is implemented. It is important to establish some baseline rules about the amount of testing that should be carried out to ultimately satisfy the client that the solution will 'meet the requirements' and therefore be 'fit for purpose'. As with many things, this comes down to metrics.

Each requirement that the solution will be tested against needs to be agreed and signed off by both the client and the supplier prior to the commencement of the project. This can be changed under formal change control but will establish the baseline by which the solution will be 'proven' to be fit for purpose.

Each requirement needs to be:

- Quantifiable requirements. Each requirement should be specific and measurable. Therefore each requirement will have a quantifiable metric that allows the test manager to establish whether the test outcome meets the requirement or not.
- Coherency and Consistency. The project specification will contain a definition of the meaning of every essential subject matter term within the specification, does it? Is every reference to a defined term consistent with its definition?

- Context. Set the context for our project, then you can test whether the context is accurate. You can also test whether we have considered all the likely requirements within that context. The context defines:
  - The problem that we are trying to solve.
  - It contains all the requirements that we must eventually meet.
  - It contains anything that we have to build
  - It contains anything we have to change.
- Completeness: Completeness is to question whether we have captured all the requirements that are currently known or whether the requirements have been written from only one point of view. Every person views the world differently according to his own job and his own idea of what is important, or what is wrong with the current system.
- Requirement or Solution: When one of your stakeholders tells you he wants a graphic user interface and a mouse, he is presenting you with a solution not a requirement. The requirement should state what the solutions should be able to do, not how it should be able to do it.
- Once the requirements have been established the business process should be established and the scenarios within them that will form part of the test schedule.

www.ingramcontent.com/pod-product-compliance
Lightning Source LLC
Chambersburg PA
CBHW031928190326
41519CB00007B/457
9781908596901